There Are Women and . . .
There Are Women

Fr. Luigi Faccenda, O.F.M. Conv.

There Are Women and . . . There Are Women

Immaculata Press
West Covina, California

Italian original:
C'e' Donna e . . . Donna
© 1981 Edizioni dell'Immacolata
Bologna, Italy
With ecclesiastical approval

A special thanks to
John Hanrahan
and Regina Olguin
for their assistance in the review
of the English translation.

Cover by Riz Marsella

© 1993 Immaculata Press
531 East Merced Avenue
West Covina, California 91790
(818) 917-0040
ISBN 0-96259-532-2
Library of Congress Catalog Number 92-74807
Printed in the United States of America

Contents

Introduction

"Women" seems to be a very fashionable topic for reflection, research, and discussion today. Magazines, books, and other media portray this subject from the most varied points of view and philosophies of life.

There Are Women and . . . There Are Women was not born of the intention to enter into the politics of the debate nor of the presumption to be able to unfold all the richness of the mystery of women's nature and role in the world.

Rather, I thought to collect and share some of the reflections which I have developed and pondered thanks to my interaction with many women in my life as a Catholic priest and spiritual father of a consecrated family of missionary women, the Fr. Kolbe Missionaries of the Immaculata.

Women are with men the most beautiful fruit of God's creative love. Therefore, God's Revelation has been my primary source of understanding of their high dignity and mission. In Scripture, in Christ's example, and in the Church's constant teaching (especially the two Marian documents which I have quoted frequently—*Marialis Cultus* and *Mulieris Dignitatem*), I have found the inexhaustible and clear revelation of what women truly are in God's own eyes.

Moreover, a Woman has been the ideal, strength, and love of my entire life: the Blessed Virgin Mary. In her I have seen the greatness to which each woman is called by her specific nature and role.

In this book I wish to point out this living model to all women who seek to live their identity authentically. I hope also that, in the light of Mary, men will be able to see in the face of women the reflection of the original beauty of which God has gifted each and every woman when He created them in his image and likeness.

May Mary, the Woman of Nazareth, of Bethlehem, of Calvary, and of the Cenacle, complete my effort and make it fruitful.

Fr. Luigi Faccenda, O.F.M. Conv.

Chapter One

Mary: Real Model
for the Woman of Today

❧

*. . . The reality "Woman–Mother of God" . . .
determines the essential horizon of reflection on the
dignity and vocation of women. In anything we
think, say or do concerning the dignity and the vocation of women, our thoughts, hearts and actions
must not become detached from this horizon. The
dignity of every human being and the vocation corresponding to that dignity find their definitive measure in union with God. Mary, the woman of the
Bible, is the most complete expression of this dignity and vocation. For no human being, male or female, created in the image and likeness of God, can
in any way attain fulfillment apart from this image
and likeness.*

Mulieris Dignitatem, 5

The Advancement of Women
and the Feminist Movements

The advancement of women in today's world is one of the three signs of the times indicated by Pope John XXIII in his Encyclical Letter *Pacem in Terris* (39–45). The other two distinctive characteristics of our time are the socio-economic rise of the working class and the fact that all peoples have formed or are forming independent political communities.

During the last two centuries women have become ever more conscious of their fundamental equality with men and thus feel the need to overcome their inferiority complex and the demeaning conditions which dominated their relationships with men.

During this time the various feminist movements were born and exerted an ever-increasing influence. Though diversely inspired, they engaged in the battle for the civil and social promotion of women. Their goal was indicated in very decisive if ambiguous terms, like full liberation of women or feminine emancipation. They claimed absolute parity with men without due consideration of the diversity and complementariness of the two sexes.

And so slowly and with many difficulties, the door to the fields of education, scientific research, professional work, politics, leadership of industrial and commercial companies, the judiciary, diplomacy, and the military was opened to women. At the same time, the door of the home was opened and women could leave to pursue activity outside of it.

After almost two centuries women have attained the right to vote and to be elected to public office; juridical rights equal to men's; the right to work and to receive equal wages for equal work; admittance to most professions, careers, and the highest levels of education; equality and co-responsibility with men in managing family life. In this way the role of women has acquired a new dimension and women themselves have gained a new self-awareness and value. Women no longer feel subservient to men, but rather aim to live their own autonomous and free existence. They feel equal to men and demand the same rights without discrimination. They use their decision-making power and their active participation in public life and are present in almost every area of community endeavor.

This new situation has raised numerous problems of great concern to the family and society. These problems are social, economic, political, moral, spiritual, and religious and must be resolved without masculine overbearance or feminine revenge. They require the light of true principles and Faith. In this book while we will focus specifically on the religious issue of Mary and today's women this effort will shed light upon the other problems, indeed on the very issue of women's advancement.

The Issue: Mary and Today's Women

Pope Paul VI in his Apostolic Exhortation *Marialis Cultus* outlined this issue with astonishing freshness and clarity. The Holy Father noted that in our time some people have become disenchanted with devotion to the Blessed Virgin and have found it difficult to take Mary of Nazareth as a model. The Pope clearly stated that one of the causes of the difficulties experienced in devotion to the Mother of the Lord is

> The discrepancy existing between some aspects of this devotion and modern anthropological[1] discoveries and the profound changes which have occurred in the psycho-sociological field in which modern man lives and works. The picture of the Blessed Virgin presented in a certain type of devotional literature cannot easily be reconciled with today's life-style, especially the way women live today. In the home, woman's equality and co-responsibility with man in managing the family are being justly recognized by laws and the evolution of customs. In the sphere of politics women have in many countries gained a position in public life equal to that of men. In the social field women are at work in a whole range of different employments, getting further away every day from the restricted surroundings of the home. In the cultural field new possibilities are opening up for women in scientific research and intellectual activities.[2]

In other words, we may express the spiritual and religious issue of the advancement of women this way: in the past, women, considered as the angels of the home, found in the Mother of Jesus a model close to their own reality; therefore, it was natural to establish a very close relationship with her. Now, with women coming out of the home and their entrance into public life, they find it difficult to take Mary of Nazareth as a model because the horizons of Our Lady's life seem rather restricted in comparison with the vast spheres of activity open to women today. It is a matter, then, of the discrepancy between the traditional image of Mary and the modern image of women. It is a discrepancy which creates a spiritual and religious vacuum in women, who are now deprived of the luminous Marian inspiration which previously sustained them, in the Christian community in a special way.

The solution given to this problem by the pontifical document is interesting. It acknowledges the new situation in which women find themselves and even affirms that "devotion to the Blessed Virgin must also pay close attention to certain findings of the human sciences." [3] In this way it acknowledges the "modern anthropological discoveries and the profound changes which have occurred in the psycho-sociological field in which modern man lives and works." [4] Yet it also very forcefully makes two observations in regard to the image of Mary which disconcert modern women.

First observation:

First, the Virgin Mary has always been proposed to the faithful by the Church as an example to be imitated, not precisely in the type of life she led, and much less for the socio-cultural background in which she lived and which today scarcely exists anywhere. She is held up as an example to the faithful rather for the way in which, in her own particular life, she fully and responsibly accepted the will of God (cf. Lk 1:38), because she heard the word of God and acted on it, and because charity and a spirit of service were the driving force of her actions. She is worthy of imitation because she was the first and the most perfect of Christ's disciples. All of this has a permanent and universal exemplary value. [5]

Second observation:

Secondly, we would like to point out that the difficulties alluded to above are closely related to certain aspects of the image of Mary found in popular writings. They are not connected with the Gospel image of Mary nor with the doctrinal data which have been made explicit through a slow and conscientious process of drawing from Revelation.

It should be considered quite normal for succeeding generations of Christians in differing socio-cultural contexts to have expressed their sentiments about the Mother of Jesus in a way and manner which reflected their own age. In contemplating Mary and her mission these different generations of Christians, looking on her as the New Woman and perfect Christian, found in her as a virgin, wife, and mother the outstanding type of womanhood and the pre-eminent exemplar of life lived in accordance with the Gospels and summing up the most characteristic situations in the life of a woman. When the Church considers the long history of Marian devotion she rejoices at the continuity of the element of cult which it shows, but she does not bind herself to any particular expression of an individual cultural epoch or to the particular anthropological ideas underlying such expressions. The Church understands that certain outward religious expressions, while perfectly valid in themselves, may be less suitable to men and women of different ages and cultures. [6]

The Anthropological Dimension of Mariology

Having frankly explained the difficulties of the renewal of the image of Mary and devotion to her under its anthropological aspect, the Holy Father points out with as much clarity the way to achieve that renewal.

Finally, we wish to point out that our own time, no less than former times, is called upon to verify its knowledge of reality with the word of God, and, keeping to the matter at the present under consideration, to compare its anthropological ideas and the problems springing therefrom with the figure of the Virgin Mary as presented by the Gospel. The reading of the divine Scriptures, carried out under the guidance of the Holy Spirit, and with the discoveries of the human sciences and the different situations in the world today being taken into account, will help us to see how Mary can be considered a mirror of the expectations of the men and women of our time.[7]

In order to discover and to present a new image of Mary which *may be considered a mirror of the expectations of the men and women of our time*, our own time is called upon to verify its knowledge of reality with the word of God. It must, therefore, establish a method for a serious comparison between the experience of mankind and God's Revelation, two realities which should interact and yet be respected in their distinctness.

It is not enough to make reference only to the word of God and to the Church Tradition. It is also necessary to be faithful to mankind, by taking into account the discoveries of sciences and the legitimate needs of today's world. We are facing, let us say it openly, an anthropological turning point in the study of Mary's mystery.

It is not, however, a totally new method, because it has been used in former times also. Nevertheless we should recognize that contemporary theological thought has become more aware of this method, which was enacted by the Second Vatican Council [8] and feels the need to apply it in all its fields of research, particularly in those which require a necessary renewal. Among these is Mariology.

The Image of Mary: the Model of Women

The Church, throughout her history has always compared the image of Mary and the Christian concept of women, due to a profound intuition of their mutual rapport. It is not easy to present a history of these two inseparable realities and to decide which one has been stronger in different ages. One thing is certain; they have always interacted and been tightly linked.

Undoubtedly the Christian concept of women, whatever its origin might have been, became more exalted thanks to the venerable person of Mary and to the role of this Woman in the mystery of salvation. It followed that the Christian idea of women assumed a typical and transcendent importance which affected the daughters of Eve, conferring on women's virginity, motherhood, and influence a renewed value and an inexhaustible meaning.

In turn the figure of Mary comes to be understood and expressed through the idea and representation which one has of women; that is, anthropologically.

> The idea which one has of the woman is determinant in the theological field, especially in interpreting the Marian mystery. "Every age—Graef writes —identifies the figure of Mary with its own Christian ideal of womanhood." It follows that as the woman is more correctly understood, so the person and mission of the Blessed Virgin will be better understood. Therefore, the study of Mary ultimately coincides with the study of woman, since the mystery of Mary is the very mystery of femininity itself. [9]

Today's Women and Mary

Prompted by the modern image of womanhood, we will try to sketch an essential and authentic image of Mary, as proposed by the Gospel and by "the doctrinal data which have been made explicit through a slow and conscientious process of drawing from Revelation." [10]

In this way it will become evident that it is possible to compare the figure of the modern woman with that of Mary and to establish the link which necessarily unites them. Due to the limited scope of this work, we will trace the real figure of Mary and focus on her motherhood. It is this aspect, in fact, that modern women understand least and find most difficult to accept. Yet, Our Lady's motherhood always remains essential.

Everyone knows that Mary's principal title is Mother of Jesus Christ, but not everyone understands its surprising implications. This makes of her the supreme feminine ideal, with universal, although unattainable, value for all ages. We must admit that both in the reflection of theologians and in the devotion of Christian people, the concept of Mary's physical maternity was emphasized. In fact, theologians delighted in elaborating the metaphysics of the biological process of her maternity; that is, the generation in time of the Incarnate Word. Devotion, on the other hand, for the most part emphasized the bonds of love which united Mary with her Son in the restricted horizons of private family life. Naturally, modern women do not find themselves in this depiction

of Mary, confined in her private maternity, and consequently react with disaffection and disinterest toward
the Blessed Virgin.

In this book we will try to present some connotations
which may give a new vision of Mary's motherhood,
more responsive to and useful for modern women.

Notes

[1] Anthropology: the science of man; teaching about the origin, nature, and destiny of man especially from the perspective of his relation to God.

[2] Pope Paul VI, Apostolic Exhortation for the Right Ordering and Development of Devotion to the Blessed Virgin Mary *Marialis Cultus* (February 2, 1974), 34.

[3] Ibid.

[4] Ibid.

[5] Ibid., 35.

[6] Ibid., 36.

[7] Ibid., 37.

[8] Vatican Council II, Pastoral Constitution on the Church in the Modern World *Gaudium et Spes* (1965), 44.

[9] Cignelli Lino, *Maria Nuova Eva nella Patristica Greca* (Assisi: Studio Teologico "Porziuncola," 1966).

[10] Pope Paul VI, *Marialis Cultus*, 36.

Chapter Two

The Mission of Women

The personal resources of femininity are certainly no less than the resources of masculinity: they are merely different. Hence a woman, as well as a man, must understand her "fulfillment" as a person, her dignity and vocation, on the basis of these resources, according to the richness of the femininity which she received on the day of creation and which she inherits as an expression of the "image and likeness of God" that is specifically hers. The inheritance of sin suggested by the words of the Bible — "Your desire shall be for your husband, and he shall rule over you" — can be conquered only by following this path. The overcoming of this evil inheritance is, generation after generation, the task of every human being, whether woman or man. For whenever man is responsible for offending a woman's personal dignity and vocation, he acts contrary to his own personal dignity and his own vocation.

Mulieris Dignitatem, 10

In order to understand women's mission in the world and in society in the light of Faith and sound reason, one must go back to God's thought about women, seeking to interpret and evaluate the biblical texts which speak about them.

Women in the Bible

In the Bible there is more than one presentation of the nature and role of women. According to the different ages and circumstances, the biblical writings reflect varied attitudes and images.

If we compare some passages like Exodus 20:17; Deuteronomy 5:21; Proverbs 18:22, 9:13–18, 19:13–14; Sirach 36:24–27; Proverbs 31:10–31; 1 Corinthians 11:3–16, 14:34–35; 1 Timothy 2:9; we will observe that the Bible does not present archetypes, but rather figures incarnated in history and marked by the limits of history. We cannot thoughtlessly take them as points of reference or images to remember. In reading the Bible discernment is necessary; one must keep in mind its two levels: the word of God and the cultural context in which it was given, as well as the plan of God which is unfolding and men's resistance to it. Between these two levels, of course, there are often divergence and evolution.

Furthermore, one must be aware that the Bible does not speak directly about women, but about God and his plan of salvation. The Bible does treat of the vocation, mission, situation, and problems of women, but only indirectly.

We cannot study the theme *"Women"* (or many others) simply on the basis of the texts which explicitly refer to it. Our study must begin with the central biblical theme: the plan of salvation.

Finally, in the Bible we find an anthropological treatment of men and women, which comes from a particular perspective. The Bible considers man and woman as beings *in relation*, and for this reason it always speaks about them in relationship with each other, with others, and with God.

The Bible does not look at man and woman in a static way but as beings in action, as they fulfill their vocation. In other words, the Bible does not ask the question: What is woman?, but What is her vocation? What is she called to be?

The great biblical discourse on women is found in Genesis 2–3 and Genesis 1. There we find the plan of God (in which the man Adam and the woman Eve are *in dialogue*, are *images* of God, and are called to subdue the earth) and the clear awareness that this plan is now present in a historical situation marked by sin which contradicts it by causing division, domination, and self-centeredness.

The Dignity of Women in the Bible

The focal point of Genesis 2–3 is well known. Israel is looking for an answer to the problem of good and evil. On the one hand, Israel experiences the salvific love of God; and on the other, Israel experiences suffering and evil. How is it possible to reconcile these two experiences? Israel understands that one cannot blame God for the contradictions present in history. It is men's fault, for evil has a historical, not a theological, origin in freedom. Israel then reflects on the ambivalence of history: it reveals the plan of God and at the same time it hides it.

In this deep reflection on the meaning of human history, some important observations on men and women can be made. Men and women have the same dignity and are complementary to one another. The woman Eve "was taken out" of the man Adam. The biblical account, beyond its imaginative language, signifies that men and women have the same nature and the same origin. In this way one can understand their mutual attraction and the profound union which is established between them. [1]

This is the first simple and essential affirmation of women's dignity which Genesis offers us and is in striking contrast with the mentality of that time in which women were considered inferior to men. Israel itself, as its legislation testifies, was not always able to understand the significance and innovation of this affirmation. This

is an example of that divergence between the plan of
God and the mentality of his people.

In Genesis there is also another statement, dependent
on the first one, but even richer in innovation and consequences: the man Adam and the woman Eve meet in
order to overcome solitude. "It is not good for the man
to be alone" (Gen 2:18). This statement surely comes
from experience: man cannot achieve self-realization in
solitude. This experience is seen here in a religious way:
God does not abandon man to solitude; rather He calls
him to interpersonal communion. [2]

Later a profound theological motivation for this concept will be found: man cannot exist alone because he
is the image of God, Who is by his very nature love,
dialogue, and communion. [3]

The expression "I will make him a helper fit for him"
(Gen 2:18) goes far beyond the sexual sphere. It indi-
cates that the interpersonal relation is indispensable for
men in order to attain salvation. Solitude is poverty and
powerlessness, for men were not created as self-sufficient
beings.

"He [God] brought her to the man" (Gen 2:22): it is
God Himself Who brings the woman to the man. Man's
reaction is one of joyful surprise, in discovering in her
those aspects of complementarity and help which he de-
sired and could not find elsewhere.

These aspects of equality and complementarity are
also indicated by the fact that the man gives the woman

a name similar to his own. Unfortunately the Hebrew words for man and woman (*'is* and *'issah*) cannot be fully expressed in modern languages.

The whole atmosphere of the account seems to be permeated by joyful surprise. The Lord "cast a deep sleep on the man" (Gen 2:21): the narrator believes that the wonderful creative work of God does not allow spectators. Adam cannot witness the miracle of Eve's creation, but can only admire God's marvelous work as a completed event.

Eve's creation as Adam's companion is one of the great wonders of God, a mysterious and salvific deed, which continues to astound men.

Women after Original Sin

In Genesis, original sin is described as man's attempt to find fulfillment apart from God and his plan, which man finds alienating. The effect of this attempt is a self-centeredness which leads to division and domination (cf. Gen 3).

Man and woman become divided: although created to be complementary and united to each other, they accuse each other. They seek to dominate: "He [the man] shall rule over you [the woman]" (Gen 3:16). The man seeks to dominate the woman as a result of self-seeking, and competition for supremacy replaces a mutual striving for unity. God had intended dialogue, not domination. [4]

The fundamental statement expressed in Genesis 1 is that everything comes from God and is good, without dualism. Certainly in the history of mankind there is evil; however, its origin is not cosmic but historical. The root of dualism between good and evil is to be found solely in men's freedom to choose good or evil.

The text in which we are most interested is Genesis 1:26–28. The woman is created in the image and likeness of God, as is the man. Unlike the biblical description of creation found in Genesis 2:18–25, in which the man was created first and the woman was taken out of him later, the account of Genesis 1:26–28 shows that the two were created *together* and neither of the two is superior. In the beginning men and women were created equal. While in Genesis 2:18–25 complementarity seems to be one-sided (the woman created for the man), Genesis 1:26–28 removes any doubt. There is no superiority of one over the other.

The complementarity is mutual because the one *with* the other is in the image of God. They are not identical one to the other, but both are created in the image and likeness of God and *together* they are a manifestation of Him. Men and women are equal for what they have in common: activity, intelligence, love, and personhood. However, the text seems to indicate that the image of God is attained in them when what is specific and complementary to each of them becomes *communion* instead of self-seeking. [5]

We can thus conclude from reading Genesis 1–3 that men and women are complementary beings, in mutual dialogue, called to be the image of God in communion. In spite of the reality of sin and its effects throughout history, this plan of God remains on the horizon, and mankind can perceive it by vigilant discernment. [6]

No wonder there is a striking contrast between our interpretation of Genesis 1–3 and the concept of women at the time of Jesus Himself. The different rabbinic schools and contemporary religious circles had hardened the prescriptions of the law concerning women, thus affecting their social and religious situation. Women, especially the unmarried, were required for the most part to stay at home. When they left the home, they were not allowed to carry on a conversation and had to have their heads covered and their faces unrecognizable. In general they were considered to be less intelligent than men and inclined to illicit behavior irreparably marked by sexuality.

In religious matters women had only a rudimentary instruction. In the synagogues they were separated from men, but they were allowed to follow what was said and done from a porch. For all these reasons the learned Hebrew did not have many contacts with women who, among other things, were also generally suspected of sorcery. The wise man used the following prayer of praise: "Praised be the One Who did not make me a pagan, a woman, or an ignorant person!"

The Vocation of Women

In the plan of salvation a woman has her own role and her specific place where she can fulfill the mission which the Creator has assigned to her. This mission is linked to her particular psycho-physical structure and her unique personality.

Women achieve their self-realization as they respond to their vocation in one of the following states of life: married life, single life, or consecrated life.

Therefore, it is a basic requirement that women, from their adolescence and youth, learn to know themselves and to discern their vocation, by examining their own aspirations in the light of the talents received from God and by listening to God's will in their lives.

The importance of this discernment process is unfortunately proved by the sadness and frustration which women feel when they have not followed their vocation, resulting in negative consequences for their families, others, and the Church.

This human and Christian formation should start as soon as girls begin to discover the reality and problems of life. They should be led to understand that marriage is not the only vocation which fulfills their talents and their aspirations to love and to be mothers, so that they may be open to any of the above-mentioned states of life.

This work of self-knowledge and discernment should mature as they grow older. Important means to attain this end are prayer, retreats, meditation on the word of God and appropriate readings, the advice of a wise spiritual director, active participation in the Sacraments—especially the Eucharist and the sacrament of Reconciliation, a personal relationship with Mary, the events and experiences which one meets on the journey of life, and the continual attentive listening to God's voice which He never denies to those who are willing to do his will.

Notes

[1] Cf. Pope John Paul II, Apostolic Letter on the Dignity and Vocation of Women on the Occasion of the Marian Year *Mulieris Dignitatem* (August 15, 1988), 6.

[2] Ibid., 7.

[3] Ibid.

[4] Ibid., 9–10.

[5] Ibid., 7.

[6] Cf. *"Donna"* (Milan: Centro Studi U.S.M.F.—Editrice Ancora).

Chapter Three

False Impressions Concerning Women

Mary is "the new beginning" of the dignity and vocation of women, of each and every woman. A particular key for understanding this can be found in the words which the Evangelist puts on Mary's lips . . . : "He Who is mighty has done great things for me" (Lk 1:49). These words certainly refer to the conception of her Son, Who is the "Son of the Most High" (Lk 1:32), the "Holy One" of God; but they can also signify the discovery of her own feminine humanity. He "has done great things for me": this is the discovery of all the richness and personal resources of femininity, all the eternal originality of the "woman," just as God wanted her to be, a person for her own sake, who discovers herself "by means of a sincere gift of self." This discovery is connected with a clear awareness of God's gift, of his generosity. From the very "beginning" sin had obscured this awareness. . . . At the advent of the "fullness of time" (cf. Gal 4:4), when the mystery of Redemption begins to be fulfilled in the history of humanity, this awareness bursts forth in all its power in the words of the biblical "woman" of Nazareth. In Mary, Eve discovers the nature of the true dignity of woman, of feminine humanity. This discovery must continually reach the heart of every woman and shape her vocation and her life.

Mulieris Dignitatem, 11

In order to understand and appreciate better the mission of women in the light of Mary, we think it convenient and necessary to outline the identity of the *true woman*. In this way we can avoid the often repeated danger of considering women as myths divorced from reality or as the weaker sex, unable to face the problems of daily life and respond to the needs of society.

The nature and role of women has been frequently and poorly discussed. To speak ill of women is one of the easiest and most widespread pastimes, and literature abounds with sayings full of harsh judgments, irony, mistrust, and sometimes, contempt.

Sayings about Women

A pious man like St. Ambrose said: "In order to deceive a woman the serpent was needed, in order to deceive a man, a woman is enough." Nietzsche, a woman-hating genius, retorted: "Are you going in the midst of women? Do not forget the whip." Sometimes the comparison is made between women and Satan: "A woman and the devil walk the same road," wrote Ruiz de Alarcon, while one anonymous author felt: "Not even the devil is able to tie a woman's tongue."

Euripides stated: "A woman is the worst of all evils." The tender Flaubert: "A woman is a vulgar animal that man has idealized too much." A French writer, Decourcelle, added: "The woman whom one wishes to have is an angel; the one he actually has is a demon." The British Home: "Think the worst you can of a woman,

you will be hardly wrong." With smiling irony, the son
of Alexander Dumas wrote: "The woman, according to
the Bible, is the last thing God made. But He made her
on Saturday evening, when He was tired."

Chamfort, famous for his aphorisms, declared: "Wom-
en have one less cell in their brains and one more fiber
in their hearts." Schopenhauer wrote: "A woman is a
being with long hair and short ideas."

The lack of appreciation for women's intellect is con-
tagious. Lessing observed: "A woman who thinks is as
foolish as a man who uses cosmetics." And the French
Karr: "It is enough for a woman to have a face; a man
also needs a head." Paul Monelli said: "A woman is
like a money-box. We have to break her head in order
to get out the little good we ourselves have put into it."
Esiodus made this terrible statement: "He who puts his
trust in women, trusts thieves."

But the worst saying ever written was by a woman,
Lady Montague: "I am happy to be a woman, for I am
not in danger of marrying a woman." [1]

Why Are Women So Harshly Judged?

If such images of women have become popular and if
such biased and unjust opinions still obscure their role,
is it not perhaps because women have participated in
generating them by their own actions? Have they ever
betrayed their own dignity by wasting talents and de-
stroying gifts given in their very creation? Who has not
suffered seeing women who might have become bearers

of light, life, and hope, but who have willingly become instruments of sorrow and death?

This may be the case of the woman who commits adultery, ready to exploit a troubled family, manipulating a husband from his wife's love; the woman who indulges in the sad and degrading egotism of masturbation; the promiscuous woman, ready to display her body as her only value and treasure, ready to drag the man's body, heart, and soul into lust; the vain woman who steals or pushes her husband to steal in order to live beyond their means.

There is the wife who makes herself an "object" for her husband; the mother who is unable to give her children a profound and serene formation, who is silent when confronted with their problems of love, sex, or money, and who neglects to keep them far away from mortal dangers.

There are women who lie, gossip, and slander, who are envious and jealous. There are those who are self-centered, hysterical, or neurotic and those who desperately look for reassurance, affection, and people to console them.

There is also the woman cloaked with Christian piety, but self-seeking in her ministry and even in performing good works, thirsting for praise and acknowledgment. She is arrogant, divisive, independent, and presumptuous of her many or few talents and remains closed in her tower of pride. There are those who will use any deceit and any kind of friendship to be successful. Egotistical and yet ingratiating, lacking in true motherly love, they are ready to destroy anyone who opposes them.

These women may have given us a very negative impression which also might be gained by observing the covers of too many magazines, today's romance novels, and movies.

But, looking around, you may see that there are women who are generous and strong mothers, thoughtful sisters, young women who are heroically pure, faithful spouses, consecrated women caring for the sick, the orphan, the marginalized.

There are many others, unknown to the casual observer, who would amaze you, precisely because a woman has the great quality of not knowing the profundity of her power to love and the strength of her courage until confronted by trial.

Therefore, you will discover that the ideal of the *true woman* exists: the woman as God wanted her to be at the moment of her creation (Gen 2:18), as the helper of man and the mother of mankind.

Notes

[1] Cf. Vittorio Buttafava, *Una Stretta di Mano e Via* (Milan: Rizzoli Editore, 1976).

Chapter Four

Characteristics
of True Women

From the beginning of Christ's mission, women show to Him and to his mystery a special sensitivity which is characteristic of their femininity. It must also be said that this is especially confirmed in the Paschal Mystery, not only at the Cross but also at the dawn of the Resurrection. The women are the first at the tomb. They are the first to find it empty. They are the first to hear: "He is not here. He has risen, as He said" (Mt 28:6). They are the first to embrace his feet (cf. Mt 28:9). They are also the first to be called to announce this truth to the Apostles (cf. Mt 28:1–10; Lk 24:8–11).

Mulieris Dignitatem, 16

What is the ideal image of the *true woman* that women should strive to achieve? Men, more than women themselves, are able to grasp thoroughly the inexpressible greatness of "true" women. Men easily recognize and admire them. Although it is very difficult for men to depict women realistically, I will suggest a simple sketch of the "true woman."

The True Woman
. . . Is a Person of Profound Honesty

When a true woman discovers insincerity in her neighbor, she suffers because it harms the person and others. Even if sometimes she doubts the validity of her own opinion, she always strives to follow what she thinks is right and at the same time to remain open to other possibilities.

. . . Has Integrity

Sometimes she may wonder if her personality is acceptable to others, but she refuses to pretend to be different from what she is, to play a role, or to use insincere language in order to obtain approval and popularity. A true woman accepts herself as she is; she does not dislike herself. At times she may be ashamed of her actions but not of herself as a person. Her confidence springs from her philosophy of life. On some occasions she may be excessively emotional, but generally she refuses to be dominated by emotions. Therefore, one may expect her to act according to what she thinks is best, rather than to what she feels.

. . . Is Truly Feminine

But she is strong as only a woman can be. In discerning important matters she is neither sentimental nor irresolute. She perceives what may be unjust or suspect, even if she is unable to explain immediately the reason. She is sure in the values which inspire her life and will never betray them. She openly expresses her opinion whenever necessary.

. . . Is Able to Love with True Affection

A true woman is not inappropriately sentimental. She can sincerely express real affection for her neighbors whom she loves for what they are and not for what they have. Her manner is patient, kind, and forgiving. She is a joyful person. Her presence brings a sense of security and well-being since she radiates love and goodness as only a "true" woman can. [1]

. . . Cares for the Good of Those She Loves

She sacrifices herself for those she loves without self-pity. As a consequence, she has very little time to think of herself. Her love for others is constant and reaches out in concrete and spontaneous service. There is no fickleness in her affection: her faithfulness is one of the few things on which one can depend.

Her Perceptiveness
Grows with Experience

She quickly recognizes deception and the artificial but avoids criticizing anyone who is not present. She not only recoils from this kind of "moral murder" but also is deeply hurt when she hears it. On the other hand, despite the cost, she does not hesitate to point out another's fault when the good of others is at stake.

She Knows How to
Believe and How to Love

The Gospels simply and incisively present women who, on the way to Calvary and at the foot of the Cross, with serene and passionate courage, give witness to their fidelity to Christ's message.[2] This is all the more remarkable because at that very moment men deserted, betrayed, and denied Jesus. Mary and the other women's attitude toward Him, condemned and abandoned, was certainly fueled by their affectionate participation in his physical and moral suffering and by their maternal sensitivity. These reasons help explain the women's presence at Calvary, but further consideration is necessary.

I believe that women, more than men, are able to understand the logic which goes beyond demonstration and penetrates the barriers of what is visible and experimental. Women realize that neither experience nor demonstration is the only way to obtain certainty and to guarantee the truth of reality. It is precisely at this boundary that religious conviction begins and faith is born, not as a superficial feeling, but as a concrete and objective reality.

When a woman stands in this faith, she is not influenced by threats or fears. She believes fervently and enthusiastically and accepts the risk of living her faith to the end. [3]

The True Woman's Love is Unconditional

In Jesus' Passion and Resurrection, the women played a significant role. In fact, whereas uncertainty and fear held the Apostles back, the women (Mary Magdalene, Mary the mother of James, and Salome) ran to the tomb, as soon as "The sabbath was over," "As the first day of the week was dawning," "early in the morning," "while it was still dark." It is the solicitude of love that brought these women together, prompt and determined in their love for Christ.

While still wondering, "Who will roll back the stone for us?" (Mk 16:3), they boldly set out for the tomb with "the spices they had prepared" (cf. Lk 24:1). As the sun is just rising, another sun, "an angel of the Lord," appears to them. "He resembled a flash of lightning while his garments were as dazzling as snow" (Mt 28:3). And he addressed the women: "Do not be frightened. I know you are looking for Jesus the Crucified, but He is not here. He has been raised!" (Mt 28:5–6; cf. Jn 20: 11–18).

The spices, which are no longer needed, remain there

by the tomb, as paschal symbols of the unconditional, unselfish gift of self, just as was "the costly perfume made from genuine aromatic nard" with which Mary, Lazarus' sister, "anointed Jesus' feet. Then she dried . . . [them] with her hair, and the house was filled with the ointment's fragrance" (Jn 12:3).

The unused spices remain in the Church and in the world whenever a Christian, in imitation of the women's unselfish love, denies, gives, and sacrifices himself for the love of God and neighbor. In this way the spices continue to be brought to the Crucified Body of Christ which is the Church.

"The spice bearers," then, deserve a role which the masculine hardness of heart does not know: that of going back to Jerusalem in order to announce that the tomb is empty, to carry the news that Christ is risen, and to inform the disciples to go to Galilee, "where you will see Him" (Mt 28:7).

"They hurried away from the tomb half-overjoyed, half-fearful, and ran to carry the good news to his disciples" (Mt 28:8). The same promptness of love, the experience of an incredible event, and the full accomplishment of Christ's promise lead them back. They now know they are bearing something far more important than spices. They are bearers of the unthinkable announcement, the Reality which may totally transform one's life: Christ is the Living One Whom we can still meet today. If only we escape the labyrinths of our self-sufficiency, we can see his light and be led by Him (or drawn by Him) "from glory to glory" (2 Cor 3:18), as St. Paul says.

The evangelist Luke says that the women "on their return from the tomb, . . . told all these things to the Eleven and the others . . . but the story seemed nonsense and they refused to believe them" (Lk 24:9–11). An unconscious mistrust of the women prevented the disciples from remembering immediately what the Teacher had told them repeatedly. Over the centuries in the Church, sometimes we have perhaps lost that simple, fresh, essential, feminine aspect that flows from the unselfishness of love.

The True Woman Is the Mother of the Living

A fresco of Fra Angelico in the convent of St. Mark in Florence, Italy, depicts an unusual detail of the agony in the garden. While the Apostles are sleeping, Martha and Mary observe Jesus with care and affection. While the Apostles do not know what to offer but their sleep, the women offer their tears in union with Christ's agony.

Although the Gospel does not mention this detail, it is wonderful that a brilliant spirit like Angelico had this insight.

During the agony in the garden, the Apostles and the women face a test of faith and trust in their Master. The Apostles are disappointed and do not want to accept the mystery of the Passion while the women perceive that it is *the Truth*. They do not rationalize about it; they accept it with loving consent.

The Apostles, called to keep the Master company, are sleeping, while Martha and Mary keep their eyes fixed on Jesus. They support Him by their loving presence. The Gospel says that "An angel then appeared to Him from heaven to strengthen Him" (Lk 22:43). Why should we not believe that the women were also there as "consoling angels"?

Here we may see a kind of historical law: men are involved in problems and are called to control them, so much so that it seems like the world is only masculine. Yet often men, while seen as the animating symbol of reality, "sleep" and lose their way. On the contrary, women, who seem to be in the background, bring men back to reality at the right moment, help them to live, and nurture them with their humble and hidden presence.

Should the Church be rebuked for not sufficiently fostering the advancement of women, as today's society does? No, it should not. The ministerial priesthood (sacred orders) must remain masculine according to Christ's explicit will. [4] I think Fra Angelico's fresco in the convent of St. Mark, offers a profound reflection: while men are sleeping close to the Master, the women are watching. Surely, the women would not have done anything more had they wanted to be in the Apostles' place. The roles of men and women are different because their missions are different. Men and women must develop their own characteristics, the specific gifts which are proper to the masculine or feminine nature.

In the Gospel it is clear that while the Apostles (men) are in the foreground, the women are in the background, as the Blessed Virgin is. She is seldom seen, but is truly the soul of everything. In her the true Life becomes incarnate. Mary, like every woman, is not only the one who carries life, but is also the Mother of the living. Women are the loving presence of life among us. [5]

Notes

[1] Cf. John J. Evoy and Van F. Christoph, *The Real Woman in the Religious Life*, (New York: Sheed and Ward, 1967).

[2] Cf. Lk 23:27; Jn 19:25.

[3] Cf. Giorgio Basadonna, article published in *Avvenire* (Italian Catholic newspaper), April 16, 1976.

[4] Cf. Pope John Paul II, Apostolic Letter on the Dignity and Vocation of Women on the Occasion of the Marian Year *Mulieris Dignitatem* (August 15, 1988), 26.

[5] Cf. Aldo Aluffi, *Breviario della Fiducia* (Torino: Elle Di Ci, 1972).

Chapter Five

The Mystery and Greatness of Married Life

. . . Genesis 3:16 is of great significance. It implies a reference to the mutual relationship of man and woman in marriage. It refers to the desire born in the atmosphere of spousal love whereby the woman's "sincere gift of self" is responded to and matched by a corresponding "gift" on the part of the husband. Only on the basis of this principle can both of them, and in particular the woman, "discover themselves" as a true "unity of the two" according to the dignity of the person. The matrimonial union requires respect for and a perfecting of the true personal subjectivity of both of them. The woman cannot become the "object" of "domination" and male "possession."

Mulieris Dignitatem, 10

Love: The Specific Value of Matrimony

Conjugal love, because of its inner structure and requirements, demands the total, exclusive, and permanent self-giving of one spouse to the other and is irrevocably expressed by personal consent with which the intimate partnership of life and love proper to marriage is established. [1]

Love must be the foundation of marriage, allowing the free choice of the spouses to commit themselves and their future to each other. Marriage is not a curse of nature, not the result of chance, nor the product of unconscious natural forces. A man and woman do not marry only to settle down, or to reach a certain social and economic position, or to socially legitimize the exercise of sexuality.

Love is and must constitute the strength and atmosphere of the entire conjugal life. The more love is deepened, the more it becomes self-sacrificing, faithful, and continually renewed. Marriage, in fact, like every other state of life, is meant to be a dynamic reality.

Every day, marriage must be refreshed through the free and responsible demonstration of love. The spouses, by loving each other, become not a sum of two individuals but a *communion of persons*, in which the husband and wife achieve a free and mutual self-giving and help each other grow in their identity as human beings.

Love, by its very nature, has a tendency to be unconditional; it gives us a glimpse of the mystery of divine
love as it is reflected in the mystery of human love. God
is the origin of conjugal love as well as of every other
love.

"Marriage," Pope Paul VI wrote, "is the wise institu-
tion of the Creator to accomplish in mankind his design
of love." [2]

Conjugal love, as an expression of the whole person,
is fully human, that is to say, of the senses and of the
spirit at the same time; it expresses itself by tenderness
and intimate physical union, but is not merely erotic
attraction. Conjugal love is faithful and exclusive. It requires a commitment of the innermost being of the husband and of the wife; love makes each grow daily and
through them builds up society.

Marriage Is a Sacrament

The Church believes and teaches that marriage is a
sacrament. [3] It elevates husband and wife and makes
them participants in a new order of reality and values,
which is the intimate life of God Who is Love (cf. 1 Jn
4:8).

Conjugal love, accepted and approved by the Church,
to which Our Lord has entrusted the sacraments, becomes a means of union with God and an efficacious
sign of God's love. In the sacramental reality, spouses,
by loving each other and their children, love God and
also give witness to and spread his love for mankind.

Conjugal love, destined to find in marriage its true and perfect accomplishment, becomes a *sign* and an *image* of a higher love, indeed of the highest love; that is, God's love for mankind whom He calls to love Him.

Already in the Old Testament, marriage is considered a covenant established with God as a witness (cf. Mal 2:14–17), a commitment promised in the presence of God (cf. Prv 2:17), which cannot be violated without suffering the penalties that safeguard the fulfillment of the covenant itself.

The covenant of love and fidelity, which is the mystery of that communion in which God gives Himself to his children while they become his own, constitutes the central content of Revelation. This mystery was foretold in the history of Israel and definitively fulfilled in Jesus Christ.

Christ reveals to us that God's fidelity to humanity is absolute and unfailing. In fact, the Son of God assumed a human nature and by means of it united Himself forever and inseparably to the whole human family. The "new humanity," fulfilled in the Church by her fidelity to Christ, as a Bride to her Groom, becomes one with Him and in Him unites herself to God the Father. Thus, in Christ, the communion between God and mankind reaches its apex. Christian marriage is meant to be a revealing and efficacious sign of such a communion.

Each Christian has the task of being a sign of God's love in the world so as to make it visible. The Christian couple is called to be more specifically a sign of Christ's love for his Church.

In uniting themselves to each other in *the sacrament of matrimony* within the ecclesial community, the Christian spouses bring to ultimate perfection their human love, because the sacrament of matrimony *is a sign of the love between God and his people.* Christian marriage is an *efficacious sign* because it really contains that love and actually communicates it to the spouses. It is a sacrament, the "great mystery" of which St. Paul speaks in his letter to the Ephesians (5:25–32).

The bond which unites Jesus Christ to mankind in the Church cannot be broken; Christian marriage, which is the sign and the image of this bond, makes manifest the character of definitiveness and indissolubility inherent in every marriage.

For Christian spouses, this is a great and sometimes difficult mission, but it is attainable because Christ abides with them. As Christ has loved his Church and gave Himself up for her, so Christian spouses are enabled in Christ to love each other faithfully forever with mutual dedication. [4]

Modeled after and inspired by the love of Jesus Christ, married life is a typical expression of Christian life; that is, a life lived imitating Jesus Christ. As such, conjugal life is a way of sanctification in which daily duties, joys, sorrows, inevitable difficulties, prayer life, and in fact, life itself work together so that spouses may grow toward full maturity and "form that perfect man who is Christ come to full stature" (Eph 4:13).

Marriage in Salvation History

Such a vision of marriage may seem idealistic or almost utopian. However, the Bible teaches us that marriage follows the essential stages of the whole human experience: the first one, the wonderful plan of God; the second, the deviation and deformation caused by sin; and finally, salvation in the mystery of Christ.

We are no longer under the power of sin, even if it still hinders our response to God. The redemptive power of Christ and the salvific action of the Church help spouses to fulfill the mysterious design of God.

The grace of marriage springs forth from Christ's Death and Resurrection. It is a paschal grace, whose everlasting source is the Eucharistic Sacrifice of the Mass. In this holy Sacrifice Christian couples perceive for themselves and for their children the Sacrament of piety, the Sign of unity, and the Bond of love. "Authentic married love," the Second Vatican Council teaches, "is caught up into divine love and is directed and enriched by the redemptive power of Christ and the salvific action of the Church, with the results that the spouses are effectively led to God and are helped and strengthened in their lofty role as fathers and mothers." [5]

To accept Christ means to accept his Cross. Human experience gives witness to the fact that marriage entails difficulties, which often may be serious and distressful (cf. Mt 19:10–11). In today's world, such difficulties are in some respects aggravated. Mutual love no longer has the permanence it once enjoyed, and reciprocal understanding and acceptance may demand more from spouses. In these situations Christians give witness to their faith in the Cross of Christ and, mindful of the exhortation of the Apostle Paul, they will always seek the strength of charity:

> "Because you are God's chosen ones, holy and beloved, clothe yourselves with heartfelt mercy, with kindness, humility, meekness, and patience. Bear with one another; forgive whatever grievances you have against one another. Forgive as the Lord has forgiven you. Over all these virtues put on love, which binds the rest together and makes them perfect" (Col 3:12–14).

True Women Educate
Themselves to Form Their Family

If marriage is to be the complete expression of love between men and women and if they are to be worthy and valid collaborators with the creative and redemptive action of God, the Creator and Redeemer, it follows that a solid and profound preparation and formation are required. This formation involves the entire person with all the faculties of soul and body: emotions, sexuality, intelligence, and will.

Love is the inner dynamism of conjugal and family life and is commonly symbolized by the heart.

The heart is not only a vital muscular organ but also a symbol of the natural site of love and intimately involving other faculties which are related to love.

It follows that intelligence enlightened by Faith must guide, form, and discipline the heart. Such guidance, formation, and discipline should be supported by the counsel and help of the family, the Church, and society. They are the foundations for whatever vocation a woman is called to live.

A woman's formation is a gradual process. It should start during her childhood and continue in her adolescence, when her heart is like a garden open to receive the seed of goodness and true beauty.

This formation should go forward with serene and constant perseverance while she is experiencing life, with its pleasant and unpleasant events, in the family, at school, and at work.

In this way her heart, which has an unlimited power to love, will learn to give itself to others, beginning with her family, relatives, and friends, and then to everyone else. It will learn a preference for the poor, the sick, and the needy.

She should avoid being led by the impulses of her likes and dislikes which could make her selfish, self-centered, and pretentious. On the other hand, she should strive to be kind and respectful to all, without equivocation, half-measures, or expectations of human reward because true love is unconditional.

A young woman should be aware of the impulses of her spirit, intellect, will, and body which have a spiritual and/or sexual origin. In this way she can discern if her heart is free, if it is master of its sentiments, or if it has been disoriented by appearances or temptations coming from others.

This formative journey will surely be more serene and efficacious if it is directed by a firm will and supported by the help of a wise confidant. Ideally this would be the mother with whom a young woman could establish a relationship of trust, openness, and understanding. In this way, a girl, a teenager, or a young woman will be able to obtain the right answer at the right moment concerning the most delicate and fundamental questions about sexuality, love, and relationships with men and women. This help will have a positive influence on her response to her vocation and on her entire life.

Yet, in addition to a loving and knowledgeable mother, a young woman needs to complement her formation by means of solid reading, the counsel of a true friend, and the advice of a wise and holy priest.

Engagement

When a young woman reaches the right age and maturity (which vary from place to place and from person to person) and is sure she is called to the married life, she may begin looking for the right man.

Engaged couples should have maturity of body, heart, and spirit lest they make love a game. Marriage, in fact, involves many risks in the relationships between husband and wife and between parents and children. It follows that marriage presupposes a full responsibility in those who choose it.

Often a premature engagement does not result in marriage or may lead to an unsuccessful or forced marriage; it also may result in single parenthood, in other sinful situations, or even in the evil of abortion.

Moreover, a woman should carefully consider the character of the man who might become her husband; that is, his talents and gifts of body, psyche, and spirit, which combine to make up the whole person.

A man and woman should be united in identical faith and ideals, expressed and lived openly during the time of their engagement. By this, they avoid dangerous and painful disappointments after their marriage when they must walk in the same direction.

It is an illusion for a woman to believe that her example, word, and sincere love will change her future husband's religious indifference and his atheistic, agnostic, or secularistic mentality when it is not evident that he has a firm and sincere will to embrace her faith.

Of course, I do not dare to affirm that the union of two persons whose faith and ideals clash is impossible. I only say that it will be difficult to live together in peace and unity, with loyalty and fidelity to one's conscience and convictions, in their conjugal relationships and in the human and Christian formation of their children.

A woman should also consider serenely and attentively the temperament of a man, since it has a very vital effect on the couple's relationships.

In fact, a man could be an excellent Christian, a faithful fiancé, husband, and father; however, if the relationships are not guided and supported by a balanced temperament and by a character which harmonizes with the woman's, the success of their marriage is threatened and the chance of undue suffering is quite possible.

Consequently, a woman, before committing herself forever to a man, should examine closely the following: Is he violent, impulsive, weak, jealous, too self-centered, or too excitable? Is he a workaholic or a lazy person? Does he frequent questionable places and have unseemly friends?

Since it is difficult or almost impossible to find the ideal man, a woman who insists on marrying one may remain single. However, there is usually a middle road between an ideal marriage and a marriage bound to fail from the beginning. A wise woman is aware of the difference and finds light and strength to act appropriately.

Engagement and Love

Engagement is a special time of grace. A man and woman come to know each other and together prepare themselves for their marriage. The grace which God lavishes on an engaged couple assists and guides them toward the ideal of a true love in which the physical and spiritual aspects are harmoniously combined.

Every act which violates the moral law is also an act against true love. Every act, even if it is licit, which is not intended as an expression of self-giving and belonging to each other spiritually, represents a lie and ultimately a surrender to selfishness. In this way, engaged couples may understand the great divine law which reserves the complete and definite self-giving of each other for the commitment of everlasting love in marriage. Only marriage sanctions in an irrevocable and definitive way the couple's decision to belong to each other as spouses.

It follows that Catholic moral law does not approve and will never approve premarital intimate acts.

In this light it is possible to understand the moral and pedagogical meaning of chastity. *Chastity* orients sexuality to the service of its real value. In particular, chastity helps to make sexuality the means of an authentic human love, which expresses itself completely, although differently, in the vocation to married life or to virginity. Love, in fact, is not at all a spontaneous natural feeling. It is a power whose seed is extremely fragile. Its growth is a delicate process and needs to be fostered and protected from continual dangers to which it may be exposed. The risk of eroticism is one of the most serious. Not infrequently, conjugal life itself becomes nothing more than a pathetic egotism.

On the contrary, the experience of chastity, by gradually permeating one's instinct, constitutes the most dynamic education to love and an affirmation of authentic freedom.

During the period of their engagement, which should not be protracted, the engaged couple will study together the elements of conjugal love, which is by its very nature unitive and procreative. [6]

Procreation

Procreation has a fundamental value in conjugal life and has very serious consequences in relation to the family and humanity. Pope Paul VI made it the object of his Encyclical *Humanae Vitae* (on the transmission of human life), which won approval among Christian people, but was also a target of much dissent and protest.

It is not the purpose of this work to discuss this subject in detail. What matters is to emphasize that engaged couples and spouses must study procreation, a mysterious and wonderful aspect of married life, considering the "whole" person and respecting divine law.

To this end, it is necessary to undertake a patient and prolonged formative process which concerns all the different aspects of the person. This process should be carried out by men and women in the light of the Faith, by means of appropriate readings, pastoral assistance provided by the diocesan or parish marriage preparation programs, and wise spiritual direction.

The teachings of the Second Vatican Council, Pope Paul VI, and Pope John Paul II present a set of values, an overall orientation of life, and a means of true progress which must be long meditated upon and profoundly assimilated in order to stimulate Christians to develop a more exhaustive understanding of marriage and family issues. [7]

A woman will be a true bride if she is aware that life is meant to be fruitful by begetting life: not only of one child, but of many children, in a spirit of trust in divine Providence and in fully human and Christian responsibility. She will be a woman true to her calling if she does not not violate natural law by using artificial and unlawful means.

Indissolubility

Indissolubility is another aspect of marriage which must be studied, understood, and accepted during the engagement.

In fact, marriage by its very nature and according to Christ's teaching is indissoluble. Indissolubility is proper, not only to sacramental marriage, but also to every marriage.

Indissolubility is rooted in the nature of love and of the conjugal community; it is required in the rearing of children, and is a primary element of family stability.

Of course, the principle of indissolubility sometimes implies profound and painful tragedies. Yet, the tragedies and consequences caused by divorce are even more serious and painful. The innocent victims of divorce are children who are forced to witness abnormal situations, to live with other "fathers" or other "mothers," and who are often tossed from one family to the other, which may lead to multiple problems: harmful and sinful activities, evil companions, rebellion, and a sense of not being loved or wanted, which adversely affect them for life. [8]

Notes

[1] Cf. Vatican Council II, Pastoral Constitution on the Church in the Modern World *Gaudium et Spes* (1965), 48–49; Pope John Paul II, Apostolic Exhortation on the Role of the Christian Family in the Modern World *Familiaris Consortio* (November 22, 1981), 11–16.

[2] Pope Paul VI, Encyclical Letter on the Transmission of Human Life *Humanae Vitae* (July 25, 1968), 8.

[3] Cf. Council of Trent, s. 24, can. 1, Denz.

[4] Cf. Vatican Council II, *Gaudium et Spes*, 48; cf. Pope John Paul II, *Familiaris Consortio*, 55–64.

[5] Ibid.

[6] Cf. Pope Paul VI, *Humanae Vitae*, 12; Pope John Paul II, *Familiaris Consortio*, 17–35.

[7] Suggested readings on married and family life: *Gaudium et Spes*, 47–52; *Humanae Vitae*; *Familiaris Consortio*.

[8] Cf. Vatican Council II, *Gaudium et Spes*, 52.

Chapter Six

The Mystery and Greatness of Single Life

. . . *The dignity of women is measured by the order of love, which is essentially the order of justice and charity. Only a person can love and only a person can be loved. This statement is primarily ontological in nature, and it gives rise to an ethical affirmation. Love is an ontological and ethical requirement of the person. The person must be loved, since love alone corresponds to what the person is. This explains the commandment of love . . . placed by Christ at the very center of the Gospel "ethos" (cf. Mt 22:36–40; Mk 12:28–34). . . . When we say that the woman is the one who receives love in order to love in return, this refers not only or above all to the specific spousal relationship of marriage. It means something more universal based on the very fact of her being a woman within all the interpersonal relationships which, in the most varied ways, shape society and structure the interaction between all persons—men and women. In this broad and diversified context, a woman represents a particular value by the fact that she is a human person, and, at the same time, this particular person, by the fact of her femininity. This concerns each and every woman, independently of the cultural context in which she lives, and independently of her spiritual, psychological, and physical characteristics, as for example, age, education, health, work, and whether she is married or single.*

Mulieris Dignitatem, 29

It is not difficult to perceive a smile of pity and, sometimes, of contempt, when someone is speaking of spinsters.

The image is of a woman who looks older or is somewhat outdated, sad, often ready to complain, to gossip, or to speak ill of others. Frustrated women! This is the common image of those women who, for varied reasons, did not marry or dedicate themselves to the good of others through their consecration to God in an institute of consecrated life.

Behind the dull and monotonous appearances, though, the reality of tragedies, painful situations, or gestures of heroism and of total dedication reveal the heart of a mother, a spouse, a daughter, or a sister.

It is there in the women who have not abandoned their sick, elderly, or lonely parents; who take care of a brother or sister who is ill or handicapped, or has gone astray, or is without a family of his own, a job, or a guide.

There are also women acutely aware of their deficiencies who sorrowfully renounce marriage and family life in order not to disappoint and make unhappy a husband and children.

Why does the world hold these women in such contempt? Many times this conclusion is drawn from obvious prejudices or a wrong idea about life: a woman must be useful and successful, and the only way that this can be achieved is to be a wife and a mother, or a consecrated person.

But other times the world's misunderstanding is a reaction to the radical feminist mentality of women who choose to renounce marriage out of selfishness or lack of acceptance of their womanhood, or to the behavior of women who have not found the right man and then have clothed themselves in anger and jealousy.

Single life, accepted with love as a vocation, even if to all appearances it seems undertaken against one's will, is a truly great state of life, enabling women to become benefactresses of the family, society, and the Church.

In single life a woman can fully achieve self-realization if she uses her talents fruitfully and if at the end of each day, she can say to herself: Today I have helped somebody; I did good to those I approached; I gave time to prayer and to my Christian formation.

The single life, moreover, will be more sublime and complete if a woman, faithful to her calling to be a *true* woman and a generous Christian, offers God her whole heart.

In order to understand correctly the single life, it is necessary to form a public consciousness free from prejudice and a more Christian culture concerning the purpose and value of life, the mission of women, and the relationship between men and women.

This issue should be discussed with trust, respect, and mutual esteem.

Life, in itself, is never a failure, even if one does not embrace the married or consecrated life. The true failure of life is in not attaining eternal salvation, because this is the principal purpose for which God has created men and women.

Chapter Seven

The Mystery and Greatness
of Consecrated Life

By freely choosing virginity, women confirm them-
selves as persons, as beings whom the Creator from
the beginning has willed for their own sake. At the
same time they realize the personal value of their
own femininity by becoming "a sincere gift" for
God Who has revealed Himself in Christ, a gift for
Christ, the Redeemer of humanity and the Spouse
of souls: a "spousal" gift. One cannot correctly un-
derstand virginity—a woman's consecration in vir-
ginity—without referring to spousal love. . . .
   Virginity according to the Gospel means renounc-
ing marriage and thus physical motherhood. Never-
theless, the renunciation of this kind of motherhood,
a renunciation that can involve great sacrifice for a
woman, makes possible a different kind of moth-
erhood: motherhood "according to the Spirit" (cf.
Rom 8:4). For virginity does not deprive a woman
of her prerogatives. Spiritual motherhood takes on
many different forms. In the life of consecrated
women, for example, who live according to the
charism and the rules of the various Apostolic In-
stitutes, it can express itself as concern for people,
especially the most needy. . . . In this way a con-
secrated woman finds her Spouse, different and the
same in each and every person, according to his very
words: "As you did it to one of the least of these my
brethren, you did it to Me" (Mt 25:40).

Mulieris Dignitatem, 20–21

When a woman, with a gesture of love, places her hand in Christ's hand, her power becomes unlimited. By embracing the evangelical counsels of poverty, chastity, and obedience, a woman indeed places her hand in Christ's. Beware! It is a mistake to think that whoever professes these three vows is automatically an efficacious instrument for the bringing about of God's kingdom. If a woman does not commit herself diligently and constantly to becoming a *true* woman, she will simply remain just a *woman*. Christ might involve her in his divine plan. Through her, however, He will not accomplish great things for the salvation of the world. Indeed, many times she will become an obstacle and will waste her own precious energies and those of her superiors, confessors, and collaborators.

A woman who is fully aware of her vocation and her mission in the Church and in society, on the other hand, will commit herself to live her consecration authentically, so as to correspond to the gift she has received in the most perfect and generous way.

The Value of Consecration to God

Who will ever be able to understand, even partially, the beauty, the value, and the greatness of the calling to consecrated life? [1] It is in fact a mystery of divine love, the most precious pearl of his Heart, a sign of Christ's special favor.

"Then Jesus looked at him *with love* and told him, 'There is one thing more you must do. Go and sell what you have and give to the poor; you will then have a treasure in heaven. After that, come and follow Me' " (Mk 10:21).

In order to present a concrete and concise picture of a woman's consecration to God, we will refer to the doctrine of the Second Vatican Council [2] and the post-conciliar Magisterium of the Church which point out the values and the fundamental aspects of consecrated life with regard to the theological, ascetical, and pastoral points of view. [3]

Consecration to God, according to the Council, springs forth from a need and an ardent desire to offer oneself totally and unconditionally to God, loved above all else. In a new and special way the Christian makes himself over to God to serve and love Him. The words of the conciliar document *Lumen Gentium* are to be very carefully read:

The Christian who pledges himself to this kind of life [consecrated life] binds himself to the practice of the three evangelical counsels by vows or by other sacred ties of a similar nature. He consecrates himself wholly to God, his supreme love. In a new special way he makes himself over to God, to serve and honor Him. True, as a baptized Christian he is dead to sin and dedicated to God; but he desires to derive still more abundant fruit from the grace of his baptism.

For this purpose he makes profession in the Church of the evangelical counsels. He does so for two reasons: first, in order to be set free from hindrances that could hold him back from loving God ardently and worshipping Him perfectly, and secondly, in order to consecrate himself in a more thoroughgoing way to the service of God. The bonds by which he pledges himself to the practice of the counsels show forth the unbreakable bond of union that exists between Christ and his Bride the Church. The more stable and firm these bonds are, then, the more perfect will the Christian's religious consecration be. [4]

This passage shows brilliantly the sublime nature of the vocation to the consecrated life and gives the most exhaustive answer to common objections and prejudices.

Pope Paul VI, during his frequent encounters with religious orders and congregations, reconfirmed many times the special function and immutable importance of the consecrated life within the Church. The growing awareness of the laity's mission and of the universal call to holiness does not diminish the importance of consecrated life, rather it increases it.

During one of his allocutions to general superiors gathered in Rome to participate in general chapters, the Holy Father clearly stated:

This state of life distinctively characterized by the profession of the evangelical vows is a perfect way of life according to the teaching and example of Jesus

Christ. It is a state of life which keeps in mind the constant growth of charity, leading to its final perfection. In other ways of life, though legitimate in themselves, the specific ends, advantages, and functions are of a temporal nature. It follows that the profession of the evangelical counsels is a superaddition to that of the consecration which is proper to baptism. It is indeed a special consecration which perfects the former one, inasmuch as by it the follower of Christ totally dedicates and commits himself to God, thereby making his entire life a service to God alone. [5]

Another conciliar document, *Perfectae Caritatis*, on the Up-to-Date Renewal of Religious Life, offers a thorough description of consecrated life which reiterates all the teachings of the Council itself and of the traditional Magisterium of the Church. [6] The decree *Perfectae Caritatis* represents an assurance of the theological basis of consecrated life and of its high esteem in the life of the Church.

The members of each institute should recall, first of all, that when they made profession of the evangelical counsels they were responding to a divine call, to the end that, not merely being dead to sin (cf. Rom 6:11) but renouncing the world also, they might live for God alone. They have dedicated their whole lives to his service. This constitutes a special consecration, which is deeply rooted in their baptismal consecration and is a fuller expression of it. [7]

The texts quoted above and all the doctrine of the Church strengthen us in the conviction that "Consecration expresses the dynamic and religious aspect of belonging entirely to God. It is lived as a witness or *epiphany* of faith in Him, as a homage to his divine sovereignty and therefore a sacrifice of the whole person to Him." [8] For this reason we can conclude that a consecrated woman, following the example of Mary, is one who makes her life an act of worship of God and this worship a commitment of her life which consists in obedience to the will of the Father. [9] This obedience, in fact, is the only way to reach the true and the most perfect sanctification.

Consecrated Women Following in the Footsteps of Christ

A consecrated woman, according to the Tradition of the Church, is not a woman who primarily gives up man, family, the world and its values such as beauty, wealth, and pleasure. Above all, she is a person totally drawn by the beauty and love of Christ the Lord, Who becomes for her all that she seeks, loves, serves, and follows.

Virginity is by definition the longing, desire, eagerness, and almost ecstasy for Christ's love. It is this undivided love which triumphs over every other desire and expectation and calls a woman to dedicate herself exclusively to the contemplation, worship, and conquest of love personified by Christ. If this love is lacking, the supreme beauty of virginity is also lacking.

This love for Christ develops into the need to follow
Him more closely, to be with Him, and to embrace the
evangelical counsels as vows, in order to follow and im-
itate Him, Who was virgin, poor, and obedient.

> . . . All those who are called by God to the prac-
> tice of the evangelical counsels, and who make faith-
> ful profession of them, bind themselves to the Lord in
> a special way. They follow Christ Who, virginal and
> poor (cf. Mt 8:20; Lk 9:58), redeemed and sanctified
> men by obedience unto death on the Cross (cf. Phil
> 2:8). [10]

In this way a consecrated woman lives in profound
communion with Him and desires solely to stay close to
Him and experience ever more his presence. As a matter
of fact, this is the fundamental attitude which embraces
every other aspect of fulfilling one's call. Indeed, all the
rest, like the commitment to serve Him, the readiness to
go even to the farthest bounds of the earth in order to
preach his Name, only develop and deepen this mutual
presence of the Master in the disciple and of the disciple
in the Master.

All men are called "to live in Christ" and to allow
Him "to live in us" in an ever more intimate way. A vocation to the consecrated life, however, grasps with im-
mediacy and totality that invitation which re-echoes the
words addressed to the first two disciples, "Come and
see" (Jn 1:39). That invitation permeates one's deepest
self as an enlivening seed and becomes the unique source

which communicates a new and permanent dynamism to all manifestations of one's life.

Consecrated Women Are an Animating Force in the Church

The conciliar documents from which we have quoted stress with particular emphasis the ecclesial dimension of consecrated life by underlining its intimate relationship with the Church and by connecting all the essential aspects of consecrated life to that ecclesial dimension.

The following passage points out that a vocation to the consecrated life is a gift which God grants to the individual but always for the good of the whole Church.

> The teaching and example of Christ provide the foundation for the evangelical counsels. . . . They therefore constitute a gift of God which the Church has received from her Lord and which by his grace she always safeguards. Guided by the Holy Spirit, Church authority has been at pains to give a right interpretation of the counsels, to regulate their practice, and also to set up stable forms of living embodying them. [11]

Previously Pope Pius XII in his document *Sponsa Christi* elucidated the highest value of consecrated virginity, by adducing the fact that the Church, in the earliest centuries, reserved one of its most beautiful liturgical pages for "Consecration of Virgins." Recently the Second Vatican Council expressed the same appreciation of consecrated virginity by establishing for the profession of the evangelical counsels a special liturgical act joined to the highest act of worship, the Holy Sacrifice of the Mass. This is another unmistakable way to bear witness to the sacred value of consecrated life, which becomes a complete dedication of one's life to the good and service of the Church. It follows that the Church rightly expects consecrated women to bear much fruit:

> All the members of the Church should unflaggingly fulfill the duties of their Christian calling. The profession of the evangelical counsels shines before them as a sign which can and should effectively inspire them to do so. For the People of God has here no lasting city but seeks the city which is to come, and the religious state of life, in bestowing greater freedom from the cares of earthly existence on those who follow it, simultaneously reveals more clearly to all believers the heavenly goods which are already present in this age, witnessing to the new and eternal life which we have acquired through the redemptive work of Christ and preluding our future resurrection and the glory of the heavenly kingdom. [12]

This document adds the following statement which increases responsibility in each consecrated woman's conscience:

> The state of life, then, which is constituted by the profession of the evangelical counsels, while not entering into the hierarchical structure of the Church, belongs undeniably to her life and holiness. [13]

It follows that a consecrated woman, by her religious profession, becomes a sign for the Church, a sign which can and should effectively inspire all the members of the Church to fulfill enthusiastically the duties of their Christian calling. She will be such a sign to the degree to which her commitment is authentic and constant. Then she will truly be for others an incentive for doing good, an animating force, a sower of joy and hope, and an inspiration for holiness. [14]

Concretely, she must be:

—*an eschatological sign* which offers all a visible presentation of the future reality; that is, Paradise.

—*a Christ-like sign* which here on earth fulfills in the most intense way the following of Jesus, imitating the Apostles who left everything and followed Him.

—*a transcendental sign*, a reminder that definitive values are not those which we find on earth, such as wealth, success, progress, but those which are above and beyond this world.

Consecrated Women Are Free Women

A person's development coincides with his growth in freedom. A consecrated woman finds her fulfillment in achieving fullness of freedom, because her whole life, with all her powers and talents, is rooted in the salvific plan of God.

In response to the superficial objection of those who think consecrated persons are deprived of their liberty,

Pope Paul VI did not hesitate to affirm that consecrated life is bathed in freedom.

> Dear sons and daughters, you have wished by means of the practice of the evangelical counsels to follow Christ more freely. . . .[15]

It is certainly necessary to clarify the concept of freedom. Freedom means to live in the midst of present realities without allowing them to master us; to become integrated with them without being absorbed in them; to dedicate oneself wholeheartedly to the service of goodness and beauty, but with interior detachment, ready to experience even death, at the time, perhaps, when one is appreciating most the joy of living and working.

Freedom and discipline, dedication and detachment, life and death are two faces of the same coin. Psychology and Revelation agree in affirming the permanent validity of this reciprocity.

Human maturity in itself will always be a relative value since it is susceptible to continual growth, and in a lifetime no one will ever fulfill all his potential for good. Human maturity is also a relative value with respect to the tasks that one is called to carry out. One may be more mature and freer in one respect and less so in another. No matter in what area this human development has to flourish, it will always imply a passage from the state of *dependence* to that of *independence*; that is, to the interior freedom by which one is enabled to make responsible and difficult choices.

In conclusion, we can say that true freedom is the sovereignty of the Spirit over one's senses and ego, and over the realm of the flesh (cf. Gal 5:13-26) and selfishness.

A significant factor to be considered is the reality of the human person. Each human being is bound, tied-up, and almost chained to himself. Therefore, one's first freedom is to be free from self. In this way, we perceive that the religious vows of poverty, chastity, and obedience are indeed an affirmation of freedom, not its denial.

In fact, by means of the vows, the Holy Spirit, Who is within us, brings the individual to the highest and most complete freedom.

By means of the vow of *poverty*, the Spirit frees the ego from greediness for goods, wealth, and comfort.

By the vow of *chastity*, the Spirit frees the ego from its tendency to be possessive of others' affection and to have an excessive attachment for one person.

Finally, by means of the vow of *obedience*, the Spirit frees the ego from its moody attitudes, inconstancy, restlessness, and indecision in making choices.

Through obedience, one acquires the wisdom of allowing oneself to be led by Wisdom itself; that is, God. Through chastity, one learns to open oneself to love all people. Through poverty, one attains the freedom to look beyond material riches and to possess the Infinite (God), by using them as a means rather than as the goal.

The following passage from the pontifical document *Evangelica Testificatio* confirms the above conclusions:

> . . . The necessity makes itself felt, . . . of passing from the psychological level to the level which is truly "spiritual." Is not the "New Man" spoken of by St. Paul perhaps like the ecclesial fullness of Christ and at the same time the sharing by each Christian in this fullness? [16]

Consecrated Women Live and Communicate Joy

A consecrated woman who fully lives God's life here on earth is a woman who lives and radiates joy.

In fact, God is close to those who seek and invoke Him with a sincere heart, [17] He is close to those who are not enslaved by the false security of power, knowledge, and possessions. He is close to those who no longer belong to themselves and who with all their strength long for Him, acknowledged and thirsted for as the supreme and unsurpassable good. [18]

What is Christian joy?

> In essence, Christian joy is the spiritual sharing in the unfathomable joy, both divine and human, which is in the heart of Jesus Christ glorified. . . . No one is excluded from the joy brought by the Lord. The great joy announced by the angel on Christmas night is truly for all the people, both for the people of Israel then anxiously awaiting a Savior, and for the numberless

people made up of all those who, in time to come, would receive its message and strive to live by it. [19]

The Blessed Virgin Mary rejoiced, and her Magnificat became the exultant hymn of all the humble. St. Stephen, while dying and seeing the heavens open, rejoiced. St. Ignatius of Antioch and all martyrs rejoiced in risking everything for Christ. St. Francis of Assisi rejoiced and expressed his joy in "The Canticle of the Creatures." St. Thérèse of Lisieux rejoiced and showed us the courageous way of abandonment into the hands of God to Whom she entrusted her littleness. St. Maximilian Kolbe [20] rejoiced in the death bunker while, with his companions, experiencing the most excruciating agony of starvation and thirst. [21] In our days, we witness Mother Teresa of Calcutta rejoicing while treating the sores of lepers or carrying the bodies of the much scorned and marginalized homeless.

> St. Paul says, "Each must do as he has made up his mind, not reluctantly or under compulsion, for God loves a cheerful giver." He gives most who gives with joy. If in your work you have difficulties and you accept them with joy, with a big smile—in this, as in any other thing, they will see your good works and glorify the Father. The best way to show your gratitude to God and people is to accept everything with joy. A joyful heart is the normal result of a heart burning with love. [22]

Once a woman religious asked Mother Teresa why sometimes consecrated women are sad. She answered:

"It is because we are full of ourselves and God cannot fill us with his joy until we become empty of ourselves." [23]

Through this continuous radiation of joy consecrated women will truly be authentic witnesses of love, as Pope Paul VI wished:

> May your life, following her [Mary's] example, give witness to that maternal love, which should animate all those who, associated in the apostolic mission of the Church, collaborate in the regeneration of men. [24]

Moreover, he pointed out:

> The joy of always belonging to God is an incomparable fruit of the Holy Spirit, and one which you have already tasted. Filled with the joy which Christ will preserve in you even in the midst of trial, learn to face the future with confidence. [25]

Notes

[1] Consecrated life involves commitment to the practice of the evangelical counsels (by vows or other sacred ties) in religious or secular institutes.

[2] The Second Vatican Council speaks of the consecration to God in the Dogmatic Constitution on the Church *Lumen Gentium* (1964), chapter VI, and in the Decree on the Up-to-Date Renewal of Religious Life *Perfectae Caritatis* (1965).

[3] Cf. Ermanno Ancilli, O.C.D., *Vita Religiosa e Concilio Vaticano II* (Rome: Pontificio Istituto di Spiritualitá Teresianum).

[4] Vatican Council II, *Lumen Gentium*, 44.

[5] Pope Paul VI, Allocution *Magno Gaudio* (May 23, 1964).

[6] Cf. Pope Pius XII, Apostolic Constitutions *Sponsa Christi* (November 21, 1950), *Sacra Virginitas* (1954) and *Provida Mater* (February 2, 1947); cf. Pope Paul VI, Apostolic Constitution *Evangelica Testificatio* (1974). Recently Pope John Paul II wrote the Apostolic Exhortation *Redemptionis Donum* (March 25, 1984) and a Letter to all Consecrated Persons Belonging to Religious and Secular Institutes on the Occasion of the Marian Year (May 22, 1988).

[7] Vatican Council II, *Perfectae Caritatis*, 5.

[8] Elio Gambari, S.M.M., *Religious Life* (Boston: St. Paul Editions, 1986), 91.

[9] Cf. Pope Paul VI, Apostolic Exhortation for the Right Ordering and Development of Devotion to the Blessed Virgin Mary *Marialis Cultus* (February 2, 1974), 21.

[10] Vatican Council II, *Perfectae Caritatis*, 1.

[11] Vatican Council II, *Lumen Gentium*, 43.

[12] Ibid., 44.

[13] Ibid.

[14] Cf. Carlo Dolza, *Il Senso della Consacrazione Religiosa* (Torino: Elle Di Ci, 1971).

[15] Pope Paul VI, Apostolic Exhortation on the Renewal of Religious Life *Evangelica Testificatio* (June 29, 1971), 4.

[16] Ibid., 38.

[17] Cf. Pope Paul VI, Apostolic Exhortation on Christian Joy *Gaudete in Domino* (May 9, 1975).

[18] Cf. St. Thomas Aquinas, *Summa Theologica*, II–II, q. 28, aa. 1, 4.

[19] Pope Paul VI, *Gaudete in Domino*, chapters II and III.

[20] Cf. Fr. Luigi Faccenda, O.F.M. Conv., *One More Gift: Total Consecration to the Immaculata According to the Spirituality of St. Maximilian Kolbe* (West Covina, California: Immaculata Press, 1990).

[21] Cf. Pope Paul VI, *Gaudete in Domino*, chapter IV.

[22] Dorothy S. Hunt, *Love: a Fruit Always in Season — Daily Meditations by Mother Teresa* (San Francisco: Ignatius Press, 1987), 108.

[23] Cf. *Avvenire* (Italian Catholic newspaper), April 29, 1977.

[24] Pope Paul VI, *Evangelica Testificatio*, 56.

[25] Ibid., 55.

Chapter Eight

Mary's Life
and Women's Life

Grace never casts nature aside or cancels it out, but rather perfects it and ennobles it. Therefore the "fullness of grace" that was granted to the Virgin of Nazareth, with a view to the fact that she would become "Theotokos," also signifies the fullness of the perfection of "what is characteristic of woman," of "what is feminine." Here we find ourselves, in a sense, at the culminating point, the archetype, of the personal dignity of women.

Mulieris Dignitatem, 5

From all that has been said, it is clear that women may truly find themselves in the figure of Mary as presented by the Gospel. Mary becomes a mirror for women of our time, so they, in turn, may truly be in the Church and society that strong and kind presence of which we are so very much in need.

Taking inspiration from Paul VI's Apostolic Exhortation *Marialis Cultus*, [1] we will highlight some of the main events of Mary's life. Later on, we can consider them in depth in order to make wise and concrete applications. Chapter nine will develop women's primary role specifically in the light of Mary's *yes* at the Annunciation.

1. Mary, taken into dialogue with God, gives her active and responsible consent, not to the solution of a marginal problem, but to that "event of world importance," as the Incarnation of the Word has been rightly called. [2]

This can be seen as a response to the aspiration of modern women, eager to participate with decision-making power in the affairs of the community.

2. Mary's choice of the state of virginity, which in God's plan prepared her for the mystery of the Incarnation, was not a rejection of any of the values of the married state but a courageous choice which she made in order to consecrate herself totally to God. [3]

Consecrated women, in contemplating this truth, will

understand that through their consecration their maternity acquires a universal dimension, enabling them to love God totally and to embrace in their hearts all their brothers and sisters without distinction.

3. Mary of Nazareth, while completely devoted to God's will, was far from being a timidly submissive woman or one whose piety was repellent to others. On the contrary, she was a woman who did not hesitate to proclaim that God vindicates the humble and the oppressed, and removes the powerful people of this world from their privileged positions (cf. Lk 1:51–53). [4]

Mary sets an example for women involved in social fields, where they feel the obligation to take a stand against injustice. Mary is a model for consecrated women who place themselves at the service of the poor, the marginalized, the sick, without compromising truth. Finally, Mary offers herself as a paragon of a solid prayer life, nurtured by meditating on the word of God and the teaching of the Church and by studying sound Catholic theology.

4. Mary, who "stands out among the poor and humble of the Lord," [5] was a woman of strength who experienced poverty and suffering, flight and exile (cf. Mt 2:13–23).

These are situations that cannot escape the attention of women who wish to support, with the Gospel spirit, the liberating energies of man and society. [6] Mary's example will encourage women to spend themselves in the service of others, especially in those countries and situations where people's advancement is extremely urgent and must be carried out without being influenced by erroneous theories.

5. Mary clearly appears not only as a mother concerned with her divine Son, but also as a woman whose action helped to strengthen the apostolic community's faith in Christ (cf. Jn 2:1–12), and whose maternal role was extended and became universal on Calvary. [7]

Participation in the salvation of mankind requires strong faith and balanced and sound love, which is completely divorced from egoism and attitudes of possessiveness and exclusiveness. Participation in the work of salvation demands integrity of mind and a universal spirit; that is, a purity of intention which aims solely to please God and to seek the good of others.

Now that we have highlighted these considerations from the document *Marialis Cultus*, we shall expand our reflection to additional applications also suggested by the Gospel.

1. Women who prefer active initiatives in response to the real needs of others will admire the Blessed Virgin who goes "in haste" (Lk 1:39) to assist Elizabeth, her kinswoman, and feel the necessity of offering their service to those in need, beginning with those in their immediate circle.

2. Women who thirst for silence and contemplation will see in Mary the model of a life of prayer and intimate union with God, and will be able to reach the goal of a true integration of contemplation and action. This integration gives a contemplative force to action and an intention essentially active and apostolic to contemplation. [8]

3. Women who are attracted to community life will discover Mary, who lived in the first community with the Apostles, "the women . . . and with his [Jesus'] brethren" (Acts 1:14). That first community was born with Mary, and with her grew, became a witness of love, and expanded in apostolic fruitfulness. [9]

Pope Paul VI's lucid analysis clearly leads us to realize that Mary can indeed be considered a mirror of the expectations of men and women of our time and that her life, in its essential values, is a real response to those expectations.

We wish now to focus on some profound observations which will shed light on Mary's motherhood in relation to today's women who have a great role within the Church of which Mary is the type and the model.

Notes

[1] Cf. Pope Paul VI, Apostolic Exhortation on the Right Ordering and Development of Devotion to the Blessed Virgin Mary *Marialis Cultus* (February 2, 1974), 37.

[2] Ibid.; cf. St. Peter Chrysologus, *Sermo CXLIII*: PL 52, 583.

[3] Ibid.

[4] Ibid.

[5] Vatican Council II, Dogmatic Constitution on the Church *Lumen Gentium* (1964), 55.

[6] Cf. Pope Paul VI, *Marialis Cultus*, 37.

[7] Ibid.; cf. Pope Paul VI, Apostolic Constitution *Signum Magnum* (May 13, 1967), I.

[8] Cf. Fr. Luigi Faccenda, O.F.M. Conv., *Symbiosis: Contemplation and Action* (West Covina, California: Immaculata Press, 1991).

[9] Cf. Antonio Zigrossi, *Presenza di Cristo nella Comunitá Consacrata* (Milano: Editrice Ancora, 1973).

Chapter Nine

*Mary in the Mystery
of the Incarnation*

"When the time had fully come, God sent forth his Son, born of woman." With these words of his Letter to the Galatians (4:4), the Apostle Paul links together the principal moments which essentially determine the fulfillment of the mystery "pre-determined in God" (cf. Eph 1:9). The Son, the Word, one in substance with the Father, becomes man, born of a woman, at "the fullness of time." This event leads to the turning point of man's history on earth, understood as salvation history. It is significant that St. Paul does not call the Mother of Christ by her own name "Mary," but calls her "woman": this coincides with the words of the Proto-evangelium in the Book of Genesis (cf. 3:15). She is that "woman" who is present in the central salvific event which marks the "fullness of time": this event is realized in her and through her.

Mulieris Dignitatem, 3

The mystery of Mary's maternity demonstrates first of all that God wants to make a woman his first ally in the work of salvation. At the threshold of the New Covenant, the Annunciation, when God's plan of saving the world enters its definitive historical stage, God reveals to humanity that the hour has come in which the mystery of the Incarnation must be accomplished. But for this to happen, the formal consent and cooperation of humanity are necessary.

Who will ever be the representative of humanity in this pivotal moment of history? The history of the Old Covenant and the most ordinary human criteria suggest that it should have been a man, maybe the high priest. On the contrary, the gratuitous and surprising divine choice is a woman.

> One might even say that God changes his preference because He asks a woman, not a man, to participate in his design and to offer Him her contribution on behalf of humanity. The priority of the woman is explicitly acknowledged and appears to be a response to the priority which the woman had in the drama of the fall. [1]

The Second Vatican Council underlines the same concept when it comments on the Annunciation:

> The Father of mercies willed that the Incarnation should be preceded by assent on the part of the predestined mother, so that just as a woman had a share

in bringing about death, so also a woman should contribute to life. [2]

While Eve was the woman of refusal, Mary is the
woman of assent—assent to the gift of salvation and
God's grace.

> Mary is the woman who says "yes" to God. She is
> the antithesis of Eve, who in the garden said "no" to
> God and led Adam to do the same. God gave man the
> gift of freedom and so always moves human beings
> with their free cooperation. Mary is the personifica-
> tion of the assent to God and of the free acceptance of
> the divine gift. Her "fiat" at the Annunciation reveals
> clearly that she does not choose what she will do for
> God, rather she abandons herself, freely, to everything
> God's almighty Word will do in and through her. [3]

It is interesting to note that St. Luke describes the
announcement of John the Baptist's birth before that of
Jesus'. It is the same angel Gabriel who is sent from God
first to a man, the priest Zachary, then to a woman, the
Virgin Mary. But the Evangelist highlights that, while
Zachary doubted and was punished (cf. Lk 1:20), Mary
instead accepted God's message with faith and Elizabeth
proclaimed her "blessed" (cf. Lk 1:45).

In our time the world and the Church have an extreme
need of the responsible and effective *"yes" of women*.
But where can they find the perfect model of this *"yes"
to God*, which they should and wish to pronounce, if
not in Mary's fiat?

Virgin and Mother:
A Primacy of the Woman

At the Annunciation something amazing occurs. The woman, in the person of Mary, is entrusted with not only a primary role, but a unique role. The masculine partner is not present at all in the conception of the Word Incarnate. In the human birth of the Son of God, the male's participation is strictly limited. The lack of involvement of the human male in this conception might be seen as a kind of divine judgment upon him. A man does not collaborate actively in what is about to begin. Mankind is not totally excluded however: there is the Virgin Mary. In the Incarnation the male, as a specific agent of human activity and history with his responsibility as leader of humanity, is in the background, represented by Joseph. This is the Christian answer to feminism: here the woman is absolutely in the foreground, and is precisely the "*virgo*," the Virgin Mary.

The value of the virginal character of Mary's maternity is immense. It is an echo in time of the eternal generation of the Son of God and is a figure of the spiritual generation of his brethren. The virginal maternity signifies that the earthly conception and birth of the Son are to express, in the flesh, his eternal origin. The maternity of the one who shares with the Father the same first begotten Son is the echo on earth of that unique Paternity. Every masculine intervention is, therefore, inappropriate. The Son must relate only to the Father, even in his human birth. There is no greater advancement for a woman than to be associated, though in a limited manner, with the fecundity of the Father, in having the same Son the Father has.

The Second Vatican Council explains more deeply the value of this mystery of Mary's virginity and maternity when it teaches that Mary stands out as an eminent figure of the Church, both as Mother and as Virgin.

> The Church indeed contemplating her [Mary's] hidden sanctity, imitating her charity and faithfully fulfilling the Father's will, by receiving the word of God becomes herself a mother. By preaching and baptism she brings forth sons, who are conceived of the Holy Spirit and born of God, to a new and immortal life. She herself is a virgin, who keeps in its entirety and purity the faith she pledged to her Spouse. Imitating the Mother of the Lord, and by the power of the Holy Spirit, she keeps intact faith, firm hope, and sincere charity. [4]

It is a matter of giving birth in the order of grace by the working of the Holy Spirit which requires an absolute and therefore virginal union; that is, a union which is free from obstacles between the Church and Christ her Spouse. It must also be added that Mary is not only a figure of this fecundity of the Church. On the contrary, she actively participates in it, as the Council itself points out:

> The Son Whom she [Mary] brought forth is He
> Whom God placed as the first born among many
> brethren (Rom 8:29); that is, the faithful, in whose
> generation and formation she cooperates with a moth-
> er's love. [5]

St. Irenaeus called Mary "the Virgin who generates
us," so much did he see her present in the spiritual life
of the Church.

The Significance of Mary's Fiat
for the History of the World

In order to understand the tremendous influence which
Mary has exercised with her "yes" on the essential events
of history and the consequent destiny of mankind, it is
not enough to notice the priority and primacy God has
attributed to her in the accomplishment of the mystery
of the Incarnation. We must also be very attentive to her
assent and cooperation. In fact, the proposal presented
by the angelic message is not limited to the simple fact
of Mary's maternity, but it broadens to the messianic
destiny of Jesus, which is briefly described. When God
asked Mary to become the Mother of the Savior, He
called her to look far beyond the home of Nazareth. He
invited her to think of the salvation of the Jewish people
and of all humanity and to see the whole of her motherly
life in this higher universal perspective. We can truly say
that the destiny of all mankind depends on the assent
of a woman.

It is significant that God requests consent from Mary. She was asked to accept not only her motherhood but also the divine plan of salvation as expounded by the angel, who announced to her the Child's destiny and the eternal kingship He will be given. She was called to cooperate in this destiny. This means that at the Annunciation the whole work of the restoration of humanity depended on Mary's assent. This has been the most hidden and decisive of all the interventions of women in human history. In reality, the future of all people depended on Mary's attitude. Therefore, the Annunciation can be seen not only as the announcement of universal salvation, but also as a divine act which has offered women their advancement. [6]

The New Man and the New Woman

The redemptive Incarnation, however, was accomplished by the Man Jesus Christ, the only Savior of the world, as the Church recalls in the Second Vatican Council:

> In the words of the Apostle there is but one Mediator: "for there is but one God and one Mediator of God and men, the Man Christ Jesus, who gave Himself as redemption for all" (1 Tim 2:5–6). [7]

In the abstract, we may discuss all the different possibilities concerning Creation and Redemption. By faith, however, we must accept, try to understand, and live by the only real choice which corresponds to the unequivocal divine design, always one of love even though full of mystery. The unfathomable eternal plan of the Father decreed that the Son would become incarnate in the Man Jesus.

This fundamental truth of Faith should not lead theologians to such an absolute and exclusive Christocentrism as to completely confine Mary's role in the work of Redemption to the background. Though the Father has given Christ, the New Adam, the eminent and unique role which is due to the Son of God, He has placed by his side a New Eve. Of course, she is subordinated to and dependent on Him; nevertheless, her role constitutes a true cooperation with Him. God has thus established an association of the Woman Mary with the Man Christ in the work of salvation in response to the couple, the man Adam and the woman Eve, who had committed original sin.

> In Christ the mutual opposition between man and woman—which is the inheritance of sin—is essentially overcome. "For you are all one in Jesus Christ," St. Paul will write (Gal 3:28). These words concern that original "unity of the two" which is linked with the creation of the human being as male and female, made in the image and likeness of God, and based on the model of that most perfect communion of Persons which is God Himself. St. Paul states that the mystery of man's Redemption in Jesus Christ, the Son of Mary, resumes and renews that which in the mystery of Creation corresponded to the eternal design of God the

Creator. Precisely for this reason, on the day of the creation of the human being as male and female "God saw everything that He had made, and behold, it was very good" (Gen 1:31). The Redemption restores, in a sense, at its very root, the good that was essentially "diminished" by sin and its heritage in human history. [8]

One of the dominant ideas in the Marian doctrine of the Second Vatican Council is that Mary is actively associated with Christ the Redeemer in the work of salvation of humanity in a total, unique, and universal manner, although entirely dependent on Him.

> Thus the daughter of Adam, Mary, consenting to the word of God, became the Mother of Jesus. Committing herself whole-heartedly and impeded by no sin to God's will, she devoted herself totally, as a handmaid of the Lord, to the person and work of her Son, under and with Him, serving the mystery of Redemption, by the grace of Almighty God. Rightly, therefore, the Fathers [of the Church] see Mary not merely as passively engaged by God, but as freely cooperating in the work of man's salvation through faith and obedience. [9]

She lived her total consecration up to the death of Christ on the Cross:

> This union of the Mother with the Son in the work of salvation is made manifest from the time of Christ's virginal conception up to his death. [10]

Her universal saving role will last without interruption until the eternal fulfillment of all the elect:

This motherhood of Mary in the order of grace continues uninterruptedly from the consent which she loyally gave at the Annunciation and which she sustained without wavering beneath the Cross, until the eternal fulfillment of all the elect. Taken up to heaven she did not lay aside this saving office but by her manifold intercession continues to bring us the gifts of eternal salvation. By her maternal charity, she cares for the brethren of her Son, who still journey on earth surrounded by dangers and difficulties, until they are led into their blessed home. [11]

At the same time, the Council specifies:

This, however, is so understood that it neither takes away anything from nor adds anything to the dignity and efficacy of Christ the one Mediator. No creature could ever be counted along with the Incarnate Word and Redeemer; but just as the priesthood of Christ is shared in various ways by both his ministers and the faithful, and as the one goodness of God is radiated in different ways among his creatures, so also the unique mediation of the Redeemer does not exclude but rather gives rise to a manifold cooperation which is but a sharing in this one source.

The Church does not hesitate to profess this subordinate role of Mary, which she constantly experiences and recommends to the heartfelt attention of the faithful, so that encouraged by this maternal help they may the more closely adhere to the Mediator and Redeemer. [12]

This clarification given by the Council signifies that between Christ the Savior and Mary there is no dualism or competition, but full harmony. Mary is wholly relative to Christ: He is the source, the reason, and the goal of everything she has and does. However, this total dependence, lived in total communion, must not be seen as a state of inferiority of women in relation to men, but as the supreme self-realization of Mary, simple woman, in Christ, the Son of God made man. In fact, He alone can give meaning and value to each person, male or female.

A Contribution of Complementarity

After having considered Mary's active association with Christ in the redemptive work, and after having explained that she receives all her perfection of grace from Him and depends on Him in the exercise of her feminine mission, we now examine how her specific contribution to the work of the Savior can be described. We do not hesitate to define it as a contribution of complementarity.

> . . . Mary became not only the "nursing mother" of the Son of Man but also the "associate of unique nobility" of the Messiah and Redeemer. . . . She advanced in her pilgrimage of faith, and in this pilgrimage to the foot of the Cross there was simultaneously accomplished her maternal cooperation with the Savior's whole mission through her actions and sufferings.

Along the path of this collaboration with the work
of her Son, the Redeemer, Mary's motherhood itself
underwent a singular transformation, becoming ever
more imbued with "burning charity" towards all those
to whom Christ's mission was directed.

Through this "burning charity," which sought to
achieve, in union with Christ, the restoration of "supernatural life to souls," Mary entered in a way all her
own, into the one mediation "between God and men"
which is the mediation of the Man Christ Jesus. If she
was the first to experience within herself the supernatural consequences of this one mediation—in the Annunciation she had been greeted as "full of grace"—
then we must say that through this fullness of grace
and supernatural life she was especially predisposed
to cooperation with Christ, the one Mediator of human salvation. And such cooperation is precisely this
mediation subordinated to the mediation of Christ. In
Mary's case we have a special and exceptional mediation, based upon her "fullness of grace," which was expressed in the complete willingness of the "handmaid
of the Lord." In response to this interior willingness
of his Mother, Jesus Christ prepared her ever more
completely to become for all people their "Mother in
the order of grace." [13]

Let us not forget that in God's plan the integral human
being is made up of two essential components, one masculine and another feminine, called to exist and work
together and enabled only together to mirror God's image. Men and women are indissolubly united as two

complementary aspects of the same human reality and
of the same image of God.

Therefore, in the Incarnation the woman could not
remain in the background: Mary has a role complementary to Christ. She may be seen as his complement in humanity. She certainly received her fullness of grace from
Him, but she received it in her feminine nature. In her,
God found that aspect of humanity which He did not
put on when He became a man. Although his grace has
all the qualities which it may express in a woman's soul,
these qualities could not be expressed in Him as a man.
In Mary, Christ's grace manifested itself with sentiments
and actions which could not be expressed by Christ and
his role as a man.

Jesus is the Man in Whom God's perfection was manifested in masculine traits. This perfection was to be manifested also in the woman, in feminine traits. Although
Christ's redemptive mission is addressed to both men
and women, He, being a man, could not offer women,
spouses and mothers, a model corresponding to all the
details of their condition. Undoubtedly, this explains
why Christian reflection began to compare the sinful
couple Adam–Eve with the redeeming couple Second
Adam–New Eve. This link reflects the unity of the human being (*homo*) by means of the complementarity of
the two sexes. At the same time this link pays homage to
women by associating them, according to their nature,
with the Redemption.

The profound reality of God—his perfection, holiness, goodness, and beauty—would not be completely revealed in a human form without the woman. The work of salvation is fully manifested by the cooperation of men and women. Women are, therefore, irreplaceable in the history of salvation. "Such is the theological dimension of womanhood revealed in Mary. Women, by their very being, are necessary in order to reveal the intimate mystery of God." [14]

Should one ask if the woman would have to be necessarily Mary, we would respond that our method of research is not one of abstract speculations on the many hypothetical plans by which God could have accomplished our salvation. Rather, we are concerned with the reflection on the specific historical design which God has chosen and actually fulfilled. Therefore, Revelation and the doctrinal data which have been derived from it through tedious and serious explanatory work, teach us that "the revered Mother of God, from all eternity joined in a hidden way with Jesus Christ in one and the same decree of predestination," [15] was on this earth the perfect type and model of woman—virgin, spouse, and mother.

Pope Paul VI in his *Marialis Cultus* emphasized this reality:

> It should be considered quite normal for succeeding generations of Christians in differing socio-cultural context to have expressed their sentiments about the

Mother of Jesus in a way and manner which reflected
their own age. In contemplating Mary and her mission
these different generations of Christians, looking on
her as the New Woman and perfect Christian, found in
her as a virgin, wife, and mother the outstanding type
of womanhood and the pre-eminent exemplar of life
lived in accordance with the Gospels and summing
up the most characteristic situations in the life of a
woman. [16]

Notes

1 J. Galot, *Culto Mariano e Emancipazione della Donna*, in La Civiltá Cattolica (1970), II, 123–132.

2 Vatican Council II, Dogmatic Constitution on the Church *Lumen Gentium* (1964), 56.

3 A. Feuillet, *Jésus et Sa Mère d'Après les Récits Lucaniens de l'Enfance et d'Après Saint Jean* (Paris: Gabalda, 1974).

4 Vatican Council II, *Lumen Gentium*, 64.

5 Ibid., 63.

6 J. Galot, *Culto Mariano e Emancipazione della Donna*.

7 Vatican Council II, *Lumen Gentium*, 60.

8 Pope John Paul II, Apostolic Letter on the Dignity and Vocation of Women on the Occasion of the Marian Year *Mulieris Dignitatem* (August 15, 1988), 11.

9 Vatican Council II, *Lumen Gentium*, 56.

10 Ibid., 57.

11 Ibid., 62.

12 Ibid.

13 Pope John Paul II, Encyclical Letter on the Blessed Virgin Mary in the Life of the Pilgrim Church *Redemptoris Mater* (March 25, 1987), 39.

14 J. Galot, *Teologia della Donna*, in La Civiltá Cattolica (1975), II, 241.

15 Pope Pius XII, Apostolic Constitution Defining the Dogma of the Assumption *Munificentissimus Deus* (November 1, 1950), 40.

16 Pope Paul VI, Apostolic Exhortation for the Right Ordering and Development of Devotion to the Blessed Virgin Mary *Marialis Cultus* (February 2, 1974), 36.

Chapter Ten

Devotion to the Blessed Virgin Mary: A Great Help for Women

Mary—the "woman" of the Bible (cf. Gen 3:15; Jn 2:4; 19:26)—intimately belongs to the salvific mystery of Christ, and is therefore also present in a special way in the mystery of the Church. Since "the Church is in Christ as a sacrament . . . of intimate union with God and of the unity of the whole human race," the special presence of the Mother of God in the mystery of the Church makes us think of the exceptional link between this "woman" and the whole human family. It is a question here of every man and woman, all the sons and daughters of the human race, in whom from generation to generation a fundamental inheritance is realized, the inheritance that belongs to all humanity and that is linked with the mystery of the biblical "beginning": "God created man in his own image, in the image of God He created him; male and female He created them" (Gen 1:27).

Mulieris Dignitatem, 2

The Church understands the immense value which the figure of Mary has for mankind.

The Catholic Church, endowed with centuries of experience, recognizes in devotion to the Blessed Virgin a powerful aid for man as he strives for fulfillment. Mary, the New Woman, stands at the side of Christ, the New Man, within whose mystery the mystery of man alone finds true light; she is given to us as a pledge and guarantee that God's plan in Christ for the salvation of the whole man has already achieved realization in a creature: in her. [1]

And Pope Paul VI stresses her role as a pledge and guarantee of God's salvation:

. . . The Blessed Virgin Mary offers a calm vision and a reassuring word to modern man. . . . She shows forth the victory of hope over anguish, of fellowship over solitude, of peace over anxiety, of joy and beauty over boredom and disgust, of eternal visions over earthly ones, of life over death. [2]

Mary's Universal Spiritual Maternity

This is the central theme of the Calvary scene recalled by St. John in 19:25–27.

Near the Cross of Jesus here stood his Mother, his Mother's sister, Mary the wife of Clopas, and Mary Magdalene. Seeing his Mother there with the disciple whom He loved, Jesus said to his Mother, "Woman, there is your son." In turn He said to the disciple,

"There is your Mother." From that hour onward, the disciple took her into his care.

Mary's participation in the drama of Calvary is part of God's design, as revealed by the prophetic words of Simeon (cf. Lk 2:35). God created humanity as a "unity of the two;" therefore, the association of the Woman Mary to the Man Christ in the redemptive sacrifice could not be lacking. Her feminine presence highlighted the value of the sacrifice of Christ and its consequences. (In the "Pietá," Christian art has been able to represent vividly the dramatic compassion of the Mother of Jesus.) Moreover, a new humanity was to be born of the tragedy of Christ's Passion, and this could not have happened without the participation of the woman, Mary.

Just as a woman gave her contribution to the birth of the New Man, Christ, so a woman had to cooperate in the birth of a new humanity, the Church. And Mary, who had given birth to Christ the Head of the Mystical Body, is the one who is to cooperate in giving birth to his members. Mary's presence at the foot of the Cross has a deep significance for the birth of the new Christian community. "At the moment of Calvary, Mary, as Mother and associate of the Savior, participates in the birth of the Church." [3]

By the words Jesus addressed to his Mother and to St. John at the supreme hour in which his redemptive mission was fulfilled, He sought to express not only a sign of filial piety, but also a more profound intention.

By those words Jesus consecrated Mary's cooperation in the work of salvation, entrusting her with a universal spiritual maternity. He manifested his will to establish a new motherhood on a higher dimension, a motherhood which partakes in his redemptive work:

> One can say that if Mary's motherhood of the human race had already been outlined, now it is clearly stated and established. It emerges from the definitive accomplishment of the Redeemer's Paschal Mystery. The Mother of Christ, who stands at the very center of this mystery—a mystery which embraces each individual and all humanity—is given as mother to every single individual and all mankind. . . . This "new motherhood of Mary" generated by faith, is the fruit of the "new" love which came to definitive maturity in her at the foot of the Cross, through her sharing in the redemptive love of her Son. [4]

This motherhood is a specifically feminine mission, which surpasses domestic horizons, for it is ordered to influence the spiritual destiny of humanity. Mary's motherhood extends to all mankind, especially to all believers. At the foot of the Cross, the beloved disciple John represented all those for whom Jesus died and to whom He gave Mary as their mother. By the words "Behold your son," Christ did not intend to bestow a privilege upon his Mother. Rather, He established a filial relationship between his Mother and his disciples which in the history of the Church has been practiced and expressed

in different ways and which can be summarized in the
words "entrusting" or "consecration" to Mary.

> [The] Marian dimension of Christian life [expressed
> in a special way precisely through this filial entrust-
> ing to her] takes on special importance in relation
> to women and their status. In fact, femininity has
> a unique relationship with the Mother of the Re-
> deemer. . . . The figure of Mary of Nazareth sheds
> light on womanhood as such by the very fact that
> God, in the sublime event of the Incarnation of his
> Son, entrusted Himself to the ministry, the free and
> active ministry of a woman. It can thus be said that
> women, by looking to Mary, find in her the secret of
> living their femininity with dignity and of achieving
> their own true advancement. [5]

Moreover, on Calvary Christ entrusted her with a responsibility and a task for the life of the Church. This
is an outstanding example of the collaboration in the
apostolate to which He calls every woman.

> The new commission entrusted to Mary is totally
> consonant with femininity and womanhood as such
> and is defined by the title Mother. This title seems to
> indicate that women will have their specific mission
> in the Church, a mission different from men's.
> On the other hand, this term, which could signify
> an office limited to family tasks, assumes a new di-
> mension in the work of salvation. Jesus, Who at Cana
> addressed Himself to his Mother in the perspective of
> this work [of salvation], definitively confirms the task

of women in building up the Church. They appear to be destined to undertake their specific responsibility which has an orientation at the same time different and complementary to the activity of men. [6]

The Doctrine of the Second Vatican Council

The Council speaks of this maternal office of Mary towards mankind in almost every page of Chapter VIII of *Lumen Gentium*, so that we may consider it as part of its fundamental doctrine. The scene of Calvary is particularly emphasized:

> Thus the Blessed Virgin advanced in her pilgrimage of faith, and faithfully persevered in her union with her Son unto the Cross, where she stood (cf. Jn 19:25), in keeping with the divine plan, enduring with her only begotten Son the intensity of his suffering, associated herself with his sacrifice in her mother's heart, and lovingly consenting to the immolation of this Victim Which was born of her. Finally, she was given by the same Christ Jesus dying on the Cross as a mother to his disciple, with these words: "Woman, behold your son" (Jn 19:26–27). [7]

This teaching echoes what Pope Pius XII had stated in his Encyclical, *Mystici Corporis*: "Thus she who corporally was the Mother of our Head, through the added title of pain and glory became spiritually the Mother of all his members." [8]

Many times the Council associates and almost identifies the concept of maternity to that of cooperation. Mary's motherhood characterizes her cooperation and shows its feminine character.

Mary, then, gives her specific contribution to the mystery of Redemption as a woman and a mother. For this reason, *Lumen Gentium* 53 incorporates St. Augustine's words: "She is clearly the Mother of the members of Christ . . . since she has by her charity joined in bringing about the birth of believers in the Church, who are members of her [the Church's] Head." [9]

The theme is clearly articulated in paragraph 61 of *Lumen Gentium*.

> She conceived, brought forth, and nourished Christ, she presented Him to the Father in the temple, shared her Son's sufferings as He died on the Cross. Thus, in a wholly singular way she cooperated by her obedience, faith, hope, and burning charity in the work of the Savior in restoring supernatural life to souls. For this reason she is a mother to us in the order of grace.

In an even more formal and concise way, in paragraph 63 the Council specifies:

> The Son Whom she brought forth is He Whom God placed as the first born among many brethren (Rom 8:29); that is, the faithful, in whose generation and formation she cooperates with a mother's love.

Therefore, the Council concludes that the Church, in her apostolic mission of giving birth to Christ in the hearts of the faithful and of fostering his growth in them, rightly looks to her who gave Him birth.

> In her life the Virgin has been a model of that motherly love with which all who join in the Church's apostolic mission for the regeneration of mankind should be animated. [10]

In regard to its extension, Mary's motherhood is seen as truly universal. The Council affirms that she "is clearly the Mother of the members of Christ" (53); defines that she "is Mother of Christ and Mother of all men, and most of all those who believe" (54); calls her, following the Fathers of the Church, "Mother of the living" (56); reminds the faithful that true devotion proceeds from true faith by which "we are moved to a filial love towards our Mother and to the imitation of her virtues" (67); finally the Council formulates the wish that the unity of humanity may be obtained with her help:

> The entire Body of the faithful pours forth urgent supplications to the Mother of God and of men that she . . . may now . . . intercede before her Son in the fellowship of all the saints, until all families of people, whether they are honored with the title of Christian or whether they still do not know the Savior, may be happily gathered together in peace and harmony into one People of God. . . . [11]

The Council also takes care to highlight the length of time of Mary's maternal role and assures us that it began

at the Annunciation and will last until all the elect enter
the heavenly homeland.

This motherhood of Mary in the order of grace continues uninterruptedly from the consent which she loyally gave at the Annunciation and which she sustained
without wavering beneath the Cross, until the eternal
fulfillment of all the elect. Taken up to heaven she did
not lay aside this saving office but by her maternal
intercession continues to bring us the gifts of eternal
salvation. By her maternal charity, she cares for the
brethren of her Son, who still journey on earth surrounded by dangers and difficulties, until they are led
into their blessed home. Therefore the Blessed Virgin
is invoked in the Church under the titles of Advocate,
Helper, Benefactress, and Mediatrix. [12]

Mother of the Church

Unfolding the full significance of these statements, we
recognize Mary as Mother of the Church. Her motherhood is not only individual and private toward each
one of the faithful, but also social and public toward
the whole of the Christian community.

The Marian title of "Mother of the Church" initi-
ated many discussions during the Council, which, therefore, avoided using this expression even though it did
somehow affirm its meaning by the following statement (which takes its inspiration from the Eighteenth-
Century document *Bulla Aurea Gloriosae Dominae* of
Pope Benedict XIV): "The Catholic Church taught by

the Holy Spirit, honors her [Mary] with filial affection and devotion as a most beloved Mother." [13] Later on, we find a similar statement in which the Church is described as meditating on her with filial devotion. [14]

Pope Paul VI, however, overruled the various objections and during his discourse at the conclusion of the third session of the Second Vatican Council, on November 21, 1964, solemnly proclaimed and invoked Mary as *Mother of the Church.*

> . . . For the glory of the Virgin Mary and for our own consolation, we proclaim the most Blessed Mary Mother of the Church—that is to say—of all the People of God, of the faithful as well as the pastors, who call her the most loving Mother. And we wish that the Mother of God should be still more honored and invoked by the entire Christian people by this most sweet title.

The presentation and veneration of Mary under the title of "Mother of the Church" highlight our relationship with her within an ecclesial horizon and shed much light on womanhood. Of course, every Christian can look upon Mary as his own Mother and can entrust his personal concerns to her in absolute filial intimacy. Most importantly, a Christian should turn to her as Mother of the Church and associate himself with her care for the growth in faith and love of the whole Christian community.

Since the Annunciation Mary's motherhood has been given to her by God as a cooperation in the kingdom of Christ. Therefore, her maternity in reference to each individual constitutes a whole with her maternity in reference to the entire Church. [15]

The fact that Mary's maternal influence extends to the whole Church and is not limited to private relationships of love and formation with the individual believers has necessarily an influence on the status of women in the Church and society. Sometimes there is a tendency to limit their role in the family and to refuse them the right to participate in public life. To acknowledge Mary's motherhood toward the Church means to recognize that women have this right.

It is extremely important for every woman that God has requested Mary's cooperation in the birth and life of the Church. In fact, this means that the participation of women in the birth, growth, and spread of the kingdom of the Son in the world is part of the Father's plan. Women have to contribute to the building up of the Church and society alongside men. In choosing Mary, God manifested that He wants the advancement of all women.

The true progression of women was inaugurated in Mary, Mother of Christ and Mother of mankind.

Notes

[1] Pope Paul VI, Apostolic Exhortation on the Right Ordering and Development of Devotion to the Blessed Virgin Mary *Marialis Cultus* (February 2, 1974), 57.

[2] Ibid.

[3] J. Galot, *Maria Immagine della Donna*, in La Civiltá Cattolica (1974), II, 226.

[4] Pope John Paul II, Encyclical Letter on the Blessed Virgin Mary in the Life of the Pilgrim Church *Redemptoris Mater* (March 25, 1987), 23.

[5] Ibid., 46.

[6] J. Galot, *La Donna e i Ministeri nella Chiesa* (Assisi: Cittadella Editrice, 1973), 190.

[7] Vatican Council II, Dogmatic Constitution on the Church *Lumen Gentium* (1964), 58.

[8] Pope Pius XII, Encyclical Letter *Mystici Corporis* (June 29, 1943), 128.

[9] St. Augustine, *De Sacra Virginitate*, 6: PL 40, 399.

[10] Vatican Council II, *Lumen Gentium*, 65.

[11] Ibid., 69.

[12] Ibid., 62.

[13] Ibid., 53.

[14] Cf. Vatican Council II, *Lumen Gentium*, 65.

[15] J. Galot, *Culto Mariano e Emancipazione della Donna*, in La Civiltá Cattolica (1970), II, 130.

Chapter Eleven

True Women:
Hope of the Future

. . . *The Church desires to give thanks to the Most Holy Trinity for the "mystery of woman" and for every woman — for that which constitutes the eternal measure of her feminine dignity, for the "great works of God," which throughout human history have been accomplished in and through her. . . . The Church gives thanks for all the manifestations of the feminine "genius" which have appeared in the course of history, in the midst of all peoples and nations; she gives thanks for all the charisms which the Holy Spirit distributes to women in the history of the People of God, for all the victories which she owes to their faith, hope, and charity: she gives thanks for all the fruits of feminine holiness. . . . Meditating on the biblical mystery of the "woman," the Church prays that in this mystery all women may discover themselves and their "supreme vocation." May Mary, who "is a model of the Church in the matter of faith, charity, and perfect union with Christ," obtain for all of us this same "grace". . . .*

Mulieris Dignitatem, 31

In the Virgin Mary, women will find the horizon of true faith, which, far from being separated from the world, is the strength, challenge, and incentive for building up the earthly city, while never losing sight of the heavenly city.

Like Our Lady, true women will be able to integrate within themselves human projects and the divine plan, the ability to look up to heaven and the courage to look down upon the most distressful realities, attentiveness to God and participation in historical events, Christian vocation and human solidarity, prayer and action, freedom and service, cross and joy, self-denial and full self-realization, mortification and life, obedience and responsibility, humility and self-respect, chastity and love, and, finally, charity and justice.

In this way they will attain the most perfect harmony and unity in order to become *whole* women who do not disappoint the hope of God and the expectations of others.

The Virgin Mary is, then, a most sublime and yet most relevant model, who has an extraordinary power of drawing us to follow in her footsteps. This power, however, is exercised on our will, not on our feelings. Yes, she is a paragon which must not be merely admired, but must be imitated. She is a fascinating yet extremely challenging model! [1]

Notes

[1] Cf. Alessandro Pronzato, "Appunti sulla Marialis Cultus" in *Milizia Mariana*, Bologna, 1975–1976.

Chapter Twelve

Women: Hope and Reality of My Journey

The moral and spiritual strength of a woman is joined to her awareness that God entrusts the human being to her in a special way. Of course, God entrusts every human being to each and every other human being. But this entrusting concerns women in a special way — precisely by reason of their femininity — and this in a particular way determines their vocation. . . . A woman is strong because of her awareness of this entrusting, strong because of the fact that God "entrusts the human being to her," always and in every way, even in the situations of social discrimination in which she may find herself. This awareness and this fundamental vocation speak to women of the dignity which they receive from God Himself, and this makes them "strong" and strengthens their vocation. Thus the "perfect woman" (cf. Prov 31:10) becomes an irreplaceable support and source of spiritual strength for other people, who perceive the great energies of her spirit. These "perfect women" are owed much by their families, and sometimes by whole nations.

Mulieris Dignitatem, 30

Jesus and Women

A few years ago I went on pilgrimage to the Holy Land. As I visited the various places I wrote in my journal the following thoughts:

> Today we moved from Judea to Galilee. We visited Bethphage, the grotto of the Our Father, the place where Jesus cried over ungrateful Jerusalem, Our Lady's tomb, the great stairs of the crusaders, and finally the garden of Gethsemane, where Judas' betrayal and Jesus' arrest took place. There we celebrated Holy Mass and meditated upon Jesus' answer to the mystery of suffering. Then we left for Nazareth and in the afternoon we stopped at Shechem, in Samaria, by Jacob's well. ". . . Jesus, wearied as He was with his journey, sat down beside the well. It was about the sixth hour [noon]. There came a woman of Samaria to draw water. Jesus said to her, 'Give me a drink'" (Jn 4:6–7).

I did not go down to the crypt of the Fourth Century Byzantine Basilica. I decided to stay by the well, where an old Orthodox monk was drawing water with a decrepit tin bucket by means of a pulley activated by a long and sturdy rope. I stayed there, almost as if waiting for the Samaritan woman. I sat there, tired from my long journey, thirsting for peace and the Infinite, anxious about those who do not accept the greatness of the message of salvation, the message of love, commitment, and unity which is the calling of all Christians.

" 'If you knew the gift of God. . . . Whoever drinks of the water that I shall give him will never thirst; the water that I shall give will become in him a spring of water welling up to eternal life. . . .' Just then his disciples came. They marvelled that He was talking with a woman" (Jn 4:10–27). I imagine and understand the astonishment of the Apostles, imbued with pharisaic prejudices, at seeing Jesus speaking with a woman. Instead, Jesus is neither hindered by those prejudices nor does He hesitate to ask her for a drink. The woman, in turn, is not frightened by the current mentality. In fact, she leaves her water jar and goes off into the town to announce the news that at the well there is a man "who told me all that I ever did. Can this be the Christ?" (Jn 4:29).

Even in this episode I can see that Jesus continued his spiritual renewal and became the promoter of women's true advancement. [1]

He called women, as He did men, to be his followers. He granted their supplications and publicly extolled their faith. His message proclaimed their liberation from past discriminations and announced the good news for women. Later He continued to ask women for a drink as He made them witnesses of his Passion and Death and apostles of his Resurrection.

The Apostles, then, continued to pass on Jesus' liberating message to women, as part of Christianity; and, therefore, women as believers and as bearers of charisms are held in high esteem and find advancement within the Church, especially if they are "martyrs" and "virgins."

Jesus, through the voice of the Church, continues to ask women for a drink, and we see them becoming exemplary mothers, spouses, and life-giving renewers of social and religious life. Throughout the centuries, Jesus asked women for a drink through the voice of the Popes, who called them to become apostles and helpers of men and of priests in the spread and defense of the kingdom of God and in the socio-political and cultural formation of the People of God (cf. Discourses of Pope Pius XII). In a special way, He asked them for a drink through the voice of the Second Vatican Council, with its "Message to Women." I like to recall here Pope Paul VI, who, describing Mary as a mirror of the expectations of the men and women of our time, asked women to participate with decision-making power in the affairs of the community, to acquire a universal vision, and to stand for the rights of the poor, the sick, and the marginalized.

My Association with Women

During my long journey through life I also sat by "Jacob's well" waiting for "the woman," and I approached her "asking for a drink." I suffered deeply in witnessing contempt for and mistrust of women and the denial of their intelligence, creative love, and role of complemen-

tarity as they sought to live their identity and to participate in various arenas of society.

On the other hand, my heart was parched by a mysterious thirst: I wanted souls to experience the strength of
Light and Truth and the help of Mary, who extends her
friendly hand to all, interceding for and mediating the
grace of her Son, because "She welcomed in her faith
and in her body the One Who is God and Man, Creator
and creature, never-setting Beatitude and Destiny of this
life" (Rahner).

I realized however, that, since Mary is both the genuine ideal of women as God wanted them to be at the
dawn of Creation, and the personification of the "true
women" of the New Creation, it was necessary to call
women to action and so I asked them: "Give me a
drink."

Give me a drink! And young women went off among
their friends and acquaintances, in their families and
parishes, to give witness that true renewal of life and of
the Church is brought about only by following Mary's
example and imploring her help.

Give me a drink! And mothers understood that Mary's
presence would strengthen the faith of their families and
build up the perseverance and convictions of their hus-
bands and children.

Give me a drink! And Sisters gave their care to the
sick, the elderly, and children, and spoke of a vigilant

and faithful Mother who sustains, comforts, accompanies, and makes every suffering fruitful.

Give me a drink! And many pure and generous women have left everything, following Mary's example and guidance, and have consecrated their lives to God through her, and now travel, work, live, and pray, so that the Heart of Mary may become the Refuge and Hope of mankind that suffers from the lack of Truth and Love and continues its search for true values. [2]

Give me a drink! Mothers, spouses, elderly and sick women, and consecrated women are journeying with me as sisters, mothers, and friends, and are supporting me by their prayers and sacrifices. I am aware that I owe my perseverance in the apostolate also to these women who gave me a drink, imitating Mary, who, by her presence at the foot of the Cross, her solidarity with Christ as He was abandoned on the Cross, her role as a mother giving birth, became a universal symbol of motherhood.

These women have opened my mind to a new understanding of Mary and have helped me to see the Virgin who was attentive to the events of history and lived by faith in the circumstances of her daily life and decisions.

I have become aware that the collaboration of women in my beautiful and challenging mission of presenting Mary to the world and of leading all to enter into a personal relationship with this Mother makes easier and more effective the battle against the forces of evil and

Satan. I have realized that women's influence in everyday life is necessary: their creativity; their ability to joyfully accept and bear trials, sorrow, and sufferings; their vitality which enlivens the weary with hope and enthusiasm for the struggle against indifference, lack of confidence, and uncertainty. I have seen women like crystals that reflect the light and communicate it unselfishly to others; they are pure and even luminous because of that light which they generously radiate with a mother's heart.

I recall an old song which says: "You, women, . . . do everything unselfishly. To you we owe our heartfelt gratitude because from you we receive life, all our joys, and the first smile."

For these reasons, I asked women for a drink and I was never disappointed.

Notes

[1] Cf. John Paul II, Apostolic Exhortation on the Dignity and Vocation of Women on the Occasion of the Marian Year *Mulieris Dignitatem* (August 15, 1988), 12.

[2] The author refers to the Fr. Kolbe Missionaries of the Immaculata, the Secular Institute for consecrated women which he founded in 1954, and which received pontifical approval on March 25, 1992.

This book can be obtained from any of the following centers:

UNITED STATES

Fr. Kolbe Missionaries of the Immaculata
Spes Nostra MI Center
531 East Merced Avenue
West Covina, California 91790
(818) 917–0040

Marytown
National MI Center
1600 West Park Avenue
Libertyville, Illinois 60048
(708) 367–7800

Maximilian Kolbe MI Center
66 School Street
Granby, Massachusetts 01033
(413) 467–9190

ITALY

Missionarie dell'Immacolata "P. Kolbe"
40044 Borgonuovo di Pontecchio Marconi Bologna
(051) 84.50.02/84.56.07

Missionarie dell'Immacolata "P. Kolbe"
Via Orazio 3
00193 Roma
(06) 32.35.415

Missionarie dell'Immacolata "P. Kolbe"
Via San Marco 70
37138 Verona
(045) 56.27.11

Missionarie dell'Immacolata "P. Kolbe"
Via Napoli 414
70123 Bari
(080) 44.44.17

Missionarie dell'Immacolata "P. Kolbe"
Casa di Esercizi
Via del Santuario 24
41042 Fiorano Modena
(0536) 83.02.08

Missionarie dell'Immacolata "P. Kolbe"
Via Lagarete 41
40040 Pian del Voglio Bologna
(0534) 98.225

Missionarie dell'Immacolata "P. Kolbe"
Via Carlo Cattaneo 96
20025 Legnano Milano
(0331) 54.67.98

Milizia Mariana
Piazza Malpighi 9
40123 Bologna
(051) 23.79.99

LUXEMBOURG

Missionnaries de l'Immaculée, P. Kolbe
Presbitére Hollerich
130, Route d'Esch
L-1471 Luxembourg
(00352) 48.19.98

ARGENTINA

Misioneras de la Inmaculada "P. Kolbe"
CC 311
7400 Olavarria Buenos Aires
(0284) 20.997

BOLIVIA

Misioneras de la Inmaculada "P. Kolbe"
CC 3
Montero Santa Cruz
(092) 21.331

Other works of Fr. Luigi Faccenda in English, Spanish, and Italian (Available through Immaculata Press):

English

One More Gift: Total Consecration to the Immaculata According to the Spirituality of St. Maximilian Kolbe, Symbiosis: Contemplation and Action

Spanish

Luces y Sombras de la Mujer, Tiempo de María, Con María hacia el Tercer Milenio, María Camino de Esperanza, Un Secreto para Descubrir, Peregrino hacia Ti, La Consagracion a la Virgen

Italian

C'e' Donna e . . . *Donna, Il Mio Amore Ha un Nome,* . . . *E Mi Segua, Ora Tocca a Voi, A Tu per Tu con Padre Kolbe, Sull Strade con Maria, A Te la Mia Preghiera, Era Mariana, Con Maria in Terrasanta, 30 Problemi e un Uomo, Maria Speranza Nostra, Consolatrice degli Afflitti, Sempre Mi Troverai, Lettere a un Adolescente, Alla Scoperta di un Segreto, Ascolta Ti Parla Padre Kolbe, La Speranza del Duemila, Ho Trovato Maria*